Relish
WALES
SECOND HELPING

Original recipes from the region's
finest chefs and restaurants.
Introduction by James Sommerin.

First Published 2014
By Relish Publications
Shield Green Farm, Tritlington,
Northumberland, NE61 3DX.
Twitter: @Relish_Cookbook

ISBN: 978-0-9575370-5-7

Publisher: Duncan L Peters
General Manager: Teresa Peters
Design: Vicki Brown
Relish Photography: Andy Richardson
www.awaywithmedia.com Twitter: @andyrichardson1
Editorial Consultant: Paul Robertson
Proofing Coordinator: Valerie McLeod
Sales: Wendy Rutterford

Front cover photograph by: Huw Jones

Printed in Slovenia on behalf of Latitude Press

Relish
PUBLICATIONS

OUR HAND PICKED RESTAURANTS

As the proud owner of a Relish cookbook, you may subscribe for your own personal Relish Rewards card which entitles you to free membership for one year.

You can access the Relish members' area on our website and find out what exclusive offers are available to you from the fantastic restaurants featured in our series of books throughout the UK.

SUBSCRIBE FOR YOUR REWARD CARD ON OUR HOMEPAGE
Simply register your name, address and title of Relish book purchased to receive your **FREE Relish Reward Card**
www.relishpublications.co.uk/relish-rewards

When you make a reservation, simply let the restaurant know that you are a member and take your card along with you.

WHAT ARE THE REWARDS?
The rewards will continue to be updated on the website so do check and keep in touch. These range from a free bottle of Champagne to free gifts when you dine. Relish will send you a quarterly newsletter with special discounts, rewards and free recipes. We are about quality not quantity!

All offers are subject to change. See the Relish website for details.

www.relishpublications.co.uk/relish-rewards

008
CONTENTS

010
CONTENTS

013
STARTERS

015
MAINS

017
DESSERTS

INTRODUCTION BY JAMES SOMMERIN

It's a great honour to have been asked to fly the flag for my country by writing the foreword for this second helping of Relish Wales.

The title has been lovingly created and showcases the very best of our beautiful land. Great chefs, great food and sumptuous dishes are all to be found within the pages of this stunning book. It makes for essential reading and I'm proud to be part of it.

As many of you know, it's not the first time that I've been a standard bearer for Wales. I represented my home country in the final of BBC's Great British Menu, which helped to raise the profile of our country's cuisine. It had a profoundly positive effect, not just for me, but for our nation as a whole.

Suddenly, diners and critics from smart metropolitan towns across the border were beating a path to Wales to find out more about our starry food. It was quite right that they should, for there is much for us to be proud of. We have a stunning larder, sensational produce and some of the brightest and most innovative chefs in the UK.

I was born in Caerleon and spent my formative years baking with my grandmother. I spent some years cooking in Scotland before returning home and joining The Crown at Whitebrook, where I achieved a Michelin star in April 2007.

During my happy years there, I watched with glee as Monmouthshire and Abergavenny became one of Britain's foremost foodie destinations. Great restaurants sprang up, the region's food festival became supremely popular and a new generation of chefs were inspired to get cooking.

There were reasons for our collective success. We were supplied by extraordinary producers, who farmed fantastic beef and lamb, flavoursome vegetables and delicious seasonal fruit. We were only ever a short drive from fantastic coastline, from which our fishermen harvest amazing sea bass and deliciously sweet lobsters. The range of ingredients available is breathtaking.

Wales has much in common with its Celtic sister, Scotland. There too, the diverse terrain lends itself to an abundant and eclectic larder. The terroir is responsible for all manner of treats, from rose veal to unique cheeses; from sea aster, samphire and kelp to clear water prawns.

Relish Wales showcases many of the extraordinary ingredients that are on our doorstep. They are put to good use by a passionate group of chefs who are proud to champion our home nation. But it's not just the restaurants that celebrate our story: in the pubs and bistros, the cake shops and coffee houses, artisans are going about their business and creating incredible food.

At the time of writing, I'm looking forward to opening my new restaurant in the Vale of Glamorgan, near Cardiff. I'm on a mission to give the region its first Michelin star. Hopefully that will breed confidence among other chefs and help to raise standards ever higher.

For many years, Wales hid its light away. Now, as the pages of Relish Wales show, there's never been a better time to shout from the rooftops.

James Sommerin

020
THE BEAUFORT ARMS
COACHING INN & BRASSERIE

High Street, Raglan, Gwent, NP15 2DY

01291 690 412
www.beaufortraglan.co.uk

Recently there has been a renaissance of old coaching inns built originally on main road routes around Britain. The Beaufort is one such inn, standing in the centre of Raglan village, half way between the market towns of Monmouth and Abergavenny with easy access to the M50 and the M4. It possesses a quintessential air given its physical and historical links with the nearby medieval Raglan Castle.

The interior boasts beams, slate floors and a large stone fireplace believed to originate from the castle itself. There are nooks and crannies to sit in and several eating areas which include the traditional lounge, modern brasserie, private dining room, an events suite and country bar, all decorated to combine the best of the old with every modern comfort.

Eliot and Jana Lewis, owners since 2002, follow the successful maxim of 'good food, good wine and ales in a relaxed informal atmosphere' which extends to the 17 individually decorated bedrooms, all providing flat screen televisions, free WiFi, tea and coffee making facilities, as well as goose down duvets and crisp, white, Egyptian cotton bed linen, enjoyed by locals, tourists and business people alike.

The Beaufort serves food almost all day, from freshly cooked breakfast and brunches, to afternoon teas, all made on the premises; from the à la carte menu to the development of casual dining, where our range of prime Welsh beef gourmet burgers, like everything else, gives respect to quality ingredients, well prepared and cooked.

Such respect is shown in our head chef's range of dishes from classic steak and ale pies and steamed sticky treacle sponge through to carefully chosen à la carte dishes with an emphasis on fresh, locally caught fish, which enhance our rosette award-winning brasserie's reputation.
Andy, our head chef, joined us from a successful military career where his appreciation of flavour and range of original global dishes reflect his foreign postings and with his Gloucestershire origins he brings an understanding of relaxed, quality, upbeat dishes.

The Beaufort could not be the inn it is without its offering of Cask Marque accredited gold standard quality beers, real ales and ciders. We support our local micro-brewery based in the castle buildings and other local cider makers. Beers may be sampled in our Country bar, or for many months of the year whilst dining on our south facing terrace or patio with breathtaking vistas of the Wye Valley.

Relish Restaurant Rewards
See page 007 for details.

Why not join us in this quintessential inn of the 21st Century where staff provides an unobtrusive but attentive service. Whether for business or pleasure, special occasion or just stopping for a coffee and a chat, the experience at the Beaufort is one to be repeated.

CATCH OF THE DAY

SERVES 4 (or 2 as a main course)

 Boomerang Bay Chardonnay (Australia)

Ingredients

The Fish

2 whole Welsh sea bass (filleted, pinned and boned; each fillet cut diagonally across width into even pieces)
2 tsp good quality olive oil
salt and pepper

The Broth

knob of butter
1 tbsp olive oil
4 king prawns (shell on)
12 Welsh mussels
12 baby clams
1 lemon (quartered)
100g samphire (*blanched*, seasoned)
100g fennel (finely sliced, pan fried and seasoned)
3 small new potatoes (cooked, sliced)
1.1 litres fish stock combined with 25ml dry white wine (reduced to 500ml)
salt and pepper

Garnish

lemon (zest)
parsley (chopped)

2 large frying pans (one with a lid)

Method

For The Fish And The Broth

Heat the butter and olive oil in one of the pans. Add the king prawns, mussels, clams, lemon wedges and vegetables. Season with salt and pepper. Fry for about a minute.

Whilst this is frying, heat the olive oil in the other pan, season the flesh side of the fish and place the fish in the oil, skin side down.

Add the wine and fish stock reduction to the first pan and cover to simmer for 2 minutes.

Turn over the fish and remove the pan from the heat. The fish will finish cooking in its own heat, giving you a nice crispy skin.

To Assemble

Arrange the dish by placing the shellfish, vegetables, lemon and broth in the bottom of your bowls, with the sea bass crowning the dish. Sprinkle with the parsley and lemon zest.

Serve immediately.

> **Chef's Tip**
> This 'Catch of the Day' dish works well with a variety of fresh caught fish from red snapper, grey mullet, locally caught sea bass to mussels. This dish also works well as a hearty main course by simply increasing the ingredients.

STUFFED CHICKEN BREAST, BACON, PANT YS GAWN, FONDANT POTATO, SHALLOTS, BROAD BEANS & RICH GRAVY

SERVES 4

Savigny-Les-Beaunes Rouge
(France)

Ingredients

Chicken

4 x 250g boneless chicken breast fillets (skin off)
8 rashers good quality, thick cut, smoked, back bacon
160g Pant Ys Gawn cheese (or other soft goat's cheese)
salt and pepper

Fondant Potatoes

4 large baking potatoes (unpeeled)
500ml chicken stock
10g butter
salt and pepper

Shallots

16 baby shallots (peeled)
2 tbsp olive oil

Rich Gravy

1 carrot (chopped)
2 sticks celery (sliced)
1 small onion (diced)
40g butter
25g flour
10g tomato purée
1½ litres brown chicken stock
gravy browning (optional)

Garnish

1 leek (cut into 5cm strips, deep fried until crispy and golden)
100g broad beans (cooked, peeled)

round, deep pastry cutter about 10-12cm
deep baking tray (enough room to fit the potatoes)

Method

For The Chicken

Butterfly each fillet and place a quarter of the cheese into each one, folding the chicken over to enclose the cheese. Lay out a piece of cling film 30cm squared, double thickness. Arrange 2 rashers of bacon (over the cling film) lengthways, front to back. Place the chicken lengthways, left to right, in the middle of the bacon. Season with salt and pepper and roll in the cling film, keeping it tight. Twist the ends to form a cylindrical shape and tie both ends with butcher's string. Repeat this with the remaining 3 fillets. Cook the chicken by simmering in water, the more gentle the heat the better. Simmer for approximately 12-15 minutes until cooked. Remove from the water and rest.

For The Fondant Potatoes

Preheat the oven to 180°C.

Press the pastry cutter into the potato, trimming off any excess. Place the potatoes into the baking tray and almost cover with the chicken stock. Place a knob of butter on each and season with salt and pepper. Bake in the oven for 45 minutes to 1 hour, until soft and golden brown.

For The Shallots

Toss the shallots in olive oil. Season with salt and pepper and roast in the oven for 20 minutes.

For The Rich Gravy

Fry the vegetables in the butter until golden brown. Add the flour and beat with a wooden spoon for 1 minute. This will give the sauce a glossy finish. Stir in the tomato purée and gradually add the stock, reducing the sauce each time until all the stock is used. Add a touch of gravy browning to give the sauce a rich, dark colour. Strain and season the sauce before serving.

Assemble the dish as shown in the photograph.

Chef's Tip

It is essential not to overcook or overheat the chicken as the cheese will melt away. You can add a little cheese by piping it onto the chicken if this happens.

If you peel the potatoes, the excess can be used to make a lovely, creamy mash.

CARAMEL CHEESECAKE

SERVES 12

Invenio Zinfandel Rosé
(California, USA)

Ingredients

Caramel Sauce

2 x 395g tins condensed milk
115g golden syrup
60g butter

Cheesecake

200g ginger nut biscuits (crushed)
75g butter (melted)
500g mascarpone cheese
2 lemons (juice of)
caramel sauce (see above)

Tuile Biscuit

115g butter (soft)
140g icing sugar (sifted)
3 egg whites
115g plain flour

Sorbet

1kg blackberry purée
250g sugar
250ml water

20cm round springform tin (lined with
baking parchment)

Method

For The Caramel

Combine the condensed milk, butter and syrup in a saucepan. Stir continuously on a low heat for approximately 10 minutes until it boils and darkens in colour. Remove from the heat and allow to cool.

For The Cheesecake (Prepare The Day Before)

Mix together the biscuits and melted butter then lightly press this into the tin and allow to cool. Combine the cheese, lemon and 405g of caramel sauce until smooth. Pour a layer of the mix onto the crumb base, then the rest of the caramel sauce followed by the remaining cheese mix. Leave overnight in the fridge.

For The Tuile Biscuit

Preheat the oven to 200°C.

Cream the butter and sugar together, slowly add the egg whites then fold in the flour. Spread a thin layer of the mix in a disc shape onto baking parchment on a baking tray. Bake in the oven for 4-5 minutes until lightly coloured around the edges. Leave for half a minute to cool slightly then mould around an egg cup or a dish to achieve your desired shape, ideally to accommodate the balled sorbet. Store in an airtight container until needed.

To Make The Sorbet

Place all the ingredients into a saucepan, stir well and gently bring to the boil. Pour the mix into a container to cool. When cold, churn in an ice cream maker and place into the freezer.

To Serve

Cut the cheesecake into 12 equal portions (or fewer portions if you are hungry!) and assemble as shown in the image. I like to paint on some melted chocolate and to serve with piped cream and a garnish of sugar shards. This is simply brown sugar melted on a very high heat to form a glazed sheet, then broken into shards.

> **Chef's Tip**
> All elements of this dish can be made the day before.

030
BOKHARA
BRASSERIE
AT COURT COLMAN MANOR

Pen-y-fai, Bridgend, CF31 4NG

01656 720 212
www.bokhararestaurant.com Twitter: @bokharabridgend

Nestled in the foothills of the Garw valley and surrounded by the Welsh countryside lies the opulent 18th Century Manor House, Court Colman Manor and its highly acclaimed AA Rosette awarded Bokhara Brasserie.

The dream child of the late Vijay Bhagotra, the Bokhara was established with the intention of bringing the real taste of 'back home' to the people of Wales. Now in the hands of his son, Sanjeev, his head chef, Sarvesh Jadon and their talented team, his dream is being kept well and truly alive.

The Bokhara delights in the fact that it dares to be different. Even though the dishes might be common place in the homes of many across India, you would be hard pressed to find them on the high streets of the UK.

In contrast, the ingredients are all local, the lamb used in the signature dish, Rara Gosht Cymru, is Welsh and the actual dish is a twist on an old Punjabi recipe and is Vijay's salute to the country he loved and fondly called his own.

Since its inception in 2001, Bokhara Brasserie has received accolades and plaudits from customers and peers alike. The Bokhara Brasserie is a destination restaurant that stands out from the rest. Nowhere else in the world will you find an award-winning Indian restaurant set in the resplendent surroundings of a stunning manor house built in 1766. The restaurant encapsulates the true meaning of the saying 'when East meets West.'

Relish Restaurant Rewards
See page 007 for details.

The quality of food, created by Sarvesh and his cooking team, together with the standard of service delivered by Sanjeev and his front of house staff, has earned the restaurant four titles of Best Restaurant in Wales at the British Curry Awards, the 'Oscars' of the Indian restaurant industry. Bokhara Brasserie is the first and only restaurant to achieve this feat in Wales.

TANDOORI JHINGA WITH SEAFOOD RICE

SERVES 4

 Veramonte Sauvignon Blanc,
(Chile)

Ingredients

20 jumbo prawns

First Marinade

2 dsp lemon juice
1 tsp salt
1 tsp white pepper
2 tsp ginger and garlic paste (quantities
¼ ginger to ¾ garlic)

Second Marinade

8 dsp natural yoghurt
½ tsp turmeric
2 tsp cumin powder
½ tsp degi mirch
1 tsp mustard oil
10g fresh coriander (chopped)

Seafood Rice

100g basmati rice
200ml fish stock
2 tbsp olive oil
2 tsp garlic paste
100g onion (chopped)
¼ tsp chilli powder
150g butter
200g cocktail prawns
200ml cream
10g fresh coriander (chopped)

To Finish

chaat masala (to sprinkle)
lemon juice (squeeze of)
fresh coriander (chopped)

Method

For The Prawns

Clean and peel the jumbo prawns, leaving the heads and tails on. Put them in the first marinade.

After 10 minutes, drain away any remaining liquid then place the prawns in the second marinade for a further 10 minutes. Push the prawns on a skewer and cook under a hot grill. Keep turning and cook them for 3-5 minutes.

> **Chef's Tip**
> For extra flavour, marinate the prawns and leave them overnight.

For The Seafood Rice

Boil the rice in fish stock until cooked. Strain then leave to cool for 10 minutes.

In a separate pan, heat the olive oil, fry the garlic, chopped onion, chilli powder and butter until brown. Fry the cocktail prawns for 10 seconds before adding the cooked rice and cream. Leave it to slowly cook for 2 minutes. Garnish with coriander before serving.

To Serve

Arrange the prawns neatly on a plate and then sprinkle on some chaat masala, lemon juice and coriander.

Place the rice in a small bowl, turn upside down and slowly pull the bowl away leaving a dome of seafood rice. Garnish with coriander.

RARA GOSHT CYMRU

SERVES 4

🍷 *Vavasour Pinot Noir*
(New Zealand)

Ingredients

Curry

500g leg of lamb (Welsh, only the best,
cut into cubes)
4 tbsp olive oil
1 dsp khara masala (3 bay leaves, 3 large
cardamoms, 3 sticks of cinnamon, all ground)
250g onions (chopped)
300g minced lamb
2 tbsp garlic and ginger paste
(quantities ¼ ginger to ¾ garlic)
250g leeks
½ tsp salt
½ tsp red chilli powder
1 tsp garam masala
1 tsp turmeric
1 tsp coriander powder
1 tsp cumin powder
250g fresh tomatoes (chopped)
50g natural yoghurt

Garnish

pilau rice
10g fresh coriander (chopped)
2 ginger pieces (*julienne* of)
1 green chilli (sliced)

Method

For The Curry

Put the olive oil in a pan and add the khara masala. Brown on a low flame and then add the chopped onions. Stir for 10 minutes until well browned. Add the cubed lamb and stir for 5 minutes. Add minced meat for 15 minutes (continue to stir) until the meat is tender.

Add ginger and garlic paste, stir again for 3 minutes. Add leek, salt, red chilli powder, garam masala, turmeric, coriander and cumin powder and cook for 3-5 minutes.

Finally, add the chopped tomato and natural yoghurt. Keep stirring for a final 15 minutes until the consistency thickens. Add a little water if necessary.

To Serve

Serve with pilau rice and garnish with fresh coriander, *julienne* of ginger and green chilli.

> **Chef's Tip**
> Put a knob of butter in a karahi (or a cooking pot) place in the oven for a minute so it is sizzling, then add the curry before serving.

CHOCOLATE SAMOSAS

SERVES 4

 Callia Malbec
(Argentina)

Ingredients

Chocolate Filling

200ml cream
150g dark chocolate
100g ground almonds
¼ tsp cinnamon

Samosa Pastry

16 spring roll wrappers (15cm square from
supermarket or Asian food store)
3 egg whites (lightly beaten)
oil (for frying)

Caramelised Banana

55g brown sugar
½ tsp vanilla essence
2 tbsp hot water
2 bananas (peeled, sliced)
knob of butter

Pistachio Kulfi

297g can condensed milk
410g can evaporated milk
300ml whipping cream
¼ tsp ground cardamom
25g ground pistachio nuts

Garnish

raspberry coulis
mango coulis

Method

For The Chocolate Filling

Bring the cream to the boil, remove from the heat and whisk in
the chocolate until well combined. Transfer to a mixing bowl
and mix in the ground almonds and cinnamon. Make sure the
mixture is dry, adding extra ground almonds if needed. Set aside
in fridge for 10 minutes.

Chef's Tip

Mash 1 banana up and add it to the chocolate mix to
produce a different flavour.

For The Caramelised Bananas

Heat the sugar, vanilla essence and water in a pan until a
caramel forms. Place the banana slices into the pan, coating
them in the caramel. Add the butter to the pan and heat for
another minute.

For The Pistachio Kulfi (Prepare The Day Before)

Pour the cream and both milks into a large pan and bring to the
boil. Simmer for 15 minutes, stirring constantly until the mixture
thickens. Stir in the cardamom, remove from heat and leave to
cool. Mix in the ground pistachio nuts and freeze for 5 hours.

For The Samosa Pastry

Lay a spring roll wrapper out. Glaze all over with egg white,
then put a large spoonful of chocolate filling in the centre.
Fold the wrapper diagonally in half to form a triangle and press
together to seal well. Gently flatten out the filling as you do so.
Brush the top with egg white and fold in half again, pressing
edges together to ensure the samosa is well sealed. Repeat with
remaining wrappers and filling.

To Serve

Deep fry the samosas in batches in hot oil (175°C) for 30
seconds. Drain on paper towels and arrange them on top of the
caramelised banana slice and a side ramekin of pistachio kulfi.
Garnish with raspberry and mango coulis.

040
BULLY'S RESTAURANT

5 Romilly Crescent, Cardiff, South Glamorgan, CF11 9NP

02920 221 905
www.bullysrestaurant.co.uk

Great food and architectural flair make Bully's a stand-out destination. The restaurant combines the best of unfussy, flavoursome dishes with a colourful and inspired interior.

The restaurant was established in 1996 by Paul Bullimore, in Llandaff. His son, Russell, joined the team in 2006 and his passion for food helped to take it to the next level.

Russell and his wife, Vicky, took over in 2008 and moved the business to Pontcanna.

The room contains innumerable talking points: a rainbow cushion here, an international rugby cap there, stylish chairs in the corner and much more besides.

The unique and original furnishings add a certain je ne sais quoi and give Bully's a wonderfully relaxed ambience.

The restaurant is a foodie's paradise with a reputation that extends throughout the country. Bully's sources the best seasonal produce from Welsh providers, which are complemented by a unique French wine list sourced from small, passionate growers.

The kitchen's skills are given full reign during regular seven-course gourmet nights, with matching wines, that are scheduled on alternate months. Lunchtime tasting menus are available daily with a selection of wines, at just £35.

Russell said: "We're one-of-a-kind. There's no other restaurant like us in Wales. We appeal to all sorts of people: from serious food enthusiasts who delight in our 2 AA Rosette cuisine to local business people, and from savvy young diners to a mature crowd."

Bully's routinely succeeds in its mission to provide great tasting food, efficient and friendly service and convivial surrounds. That recipe has proved successful, with the restaurant winning recommendations in both the Michelin and Good Food guides.

Relish Restaurant Rewards
See page 007 for details.

Classically-inspired, French cuisine with off-the-beaten-path wines are served in stylish surrounds at the unique Bully's restaurant.

TIAN OF CRAB & AVOCADO, GAZPACHO DRESSING

SERVES 4

 Reichsgraf von Kesselstatt, 2012 Josephshöfer, Riesling Kabinett, Ruwer (Germany)

Ingredients

Tian

2 beef tomatoes
200g white pasteurised crabmeat
60g crème fraîche
4g salt
1g white pepper
2 avocados
2 tsp olive oil (for drizzling)

Gazpacho Dressing

1 clove garlic (chopped)
400g cherry tomatoes (roughly chopped)
10ml white wine vinegar
3g caster sugar
3g salt
lemon juice (squeeze of)
60ml olive oil

Garnish

parsley

1 stainless steel ring 6cm diameter

Method

For The Tian

Blanch the beef tomatoes briefly in boiling water and immediately put them in a bowl of iced water. Remove the skin, cut in half lengthways and remove the seeds. Cut the tomatoes with the metal ring that you will be using to assemble the tian so it will fit perfectly on top.

Mix the crabmeat with crème fraîche and season. Peel and halve the avocados then slice thinly.

Place the avocado then the crabmeat in the metal ring and push down so it is compact. Place the beef tomato on top, making sure it is inside the ring.

For The Gazpacho Dressing (Prepare Ahead)

Place all the gazpacho ingredients, except the olive oil, in a blender, and turn on. With the motor running add the olive oil slowly. Pass through a fine sieve and chill for at least 3 hours.

To Serve

Pour the gazpacho dressing into a bowl. Place the crab in the middle of the bowl and remove the ring. Drizzle a little olive oil on top of the dressing.

Chef's Tip

Try to always use latex or vinyl gloves when touching crabmeat as the natural oils on your hands will shorten the shelf life of the crab.

WELSH RUMP OF LAMB PROVENCALE

SERVES 4

Domaine de Trevallon, Trevallon 2005, Provence (France)

Ingredients

Lamb

4 x 227g Welsh lamb rump
10ml olive oil
2g salt
1g ground white pepper

Pomme *Ecrasée*

1.2kg new potatoes (peeled)
6g fresh garlic purée
16g diced shallot
30g black olives (chopped)
3g salt
1g white pepper
10g parsley (chopped)

Ratatouille

50g onion (peeled, cut into 3cm dice)
70g yellow pepper (cut into 3cm triangle pieces)
70g red pepper (cut into 3cm triangle pieces)
70g courgette (cut into 3cm triangle pieces)
70g aubergine (cut into 3cm triangle pieces)
3g fresh thyme
3g garlic (finely chopped)
200ml tomato juice
2g salt
1g ground white pepper
45ml olive oil

Sauce Vierge

10g tomato *concasse* (made from
2 firm tomatoes)
30ml olive oil
10g shallot (finely diced)
2g rosemary
2g thyme
2g marjoram
5ml lemon juice
1g salt
1g pepper
5g black olives (chopped)

Method

For The Lamb

Preheat the oven to 240°C (non fan)

Season the lamb with salt and pepper, then seal in a hot, ovenproof pan and transfer to the oven making sure the lamb is skin side down. Cook the lamb until medium rare, approximately 15-20 minutes, depending on thickness. Set aside somewhere warm to rest. Once rested, slice each rump into 3 pieces.

> **Chef's Tip**
> All meat should be rested. As a general rule, the resting time should be the same amount of time as the cooking time.

For The Pomme *Ecrasée*

Boil the potatoes in water until just beginning to break up. Drain well. Put in pan and crush with a fork. Add the other ingredients to season.

For The Ratatouille

Sauté each vegetable in 15ml olive oil with 1g thyme and 1g garlic until it begins to soften. Cook each vegetable separately as each one will require different cooking times. Once softened, mix together in the same pan and add tomato juice then season. Cook on a low temperature until the ratatouille starts to bind. Add seasoning.

For The Sauce Vierge

Start by making the tomato *concasse*. Bring a pan of water to the boil. Put the tomato into the water for 5 seconds then plunge into iced water. Remove from the iced water, peel skin off and cut lengthways in half and half again. Remove seeds and pat dry. Cut into small dice.

Warm the olive oil in a pan with the shallot and herbs. Add lemon juice and seasoning. Warm again then add the olives. Remove from the heat and add the tomato. DO NOT BOIL!!

It is important to serve this warm, not hot.

To Serve

Place a quarter of the pomme *écrasée* at the bottom of each plate. Spoon the ratatouille at the top of the plate. Place 3 pieces of lamb onto the pomme *écrasée* and drizzle the sauce vierge around plate.

CHILLED SOUP OF RASPBERRIES, MINT & BASIL

SERVES 4

 Château Rieussec 1er Cru Sauternes, 2009, Bordeaux (France)

Ingredients

500ml Sauternes wine
170ml Cabernet Sauvignon
170g caster sugar
1 vanilla pod (split lengthways)
8g fresh mint leaves (chopped)
7g fresh basil leaves (chopped)
400g fresh raspberries

Garnish

6g mint leaves (finely chopped)

Method

(Prepare At Least 4 Hours Before Serving)

Bring the wines, sugar and vanilla to the boil then remove from the stove.

Wrap the mint and basil in a clean muslin cloth. Place the muslin in the wine mixture and leave to infuse. Heat to a temperature of 50°C, add the raspberries and place in the fridge for a minimum of 4 hours until chilled.

To Serve

Pour the chilled soup into dessert bowls. Sprinkle the finely chopped mint on top and serve immediately.

> **Chef's Tip**
> Chill down the jug and serving bowls before serving to keep the dessert as cold as possible. This dessert is best made on the day you wish to use it to make it as fresh as possible.

050
THE CLIFF RESTAURANT
AT ST BRIDES SPA HOTEL

St Brides Hill, Saundersfoot, Pembrokeshire, SA69 9NH

01834 812 304
www.stbridesspahotel.com Twitter: @stbrideshotel

Andrew and Lindsey Evans bought a 'seaside hotel' in 2000 and six years later St Brides Spa Hotel completed its transformation to become one of Wales' finest Luxury Destination Spa Hotels - envied for its location perched high above the seaside harbour village of Saundersfoot. In 2013, they won Best Place to Stay in Wales (National Tourism Awards), Hotel of the Year, Best View in the UK (Best Kept Secret awards) and Shoreline Hotel of the Year.

Sharing this journey, Toby Goodwin returned to Saundersfoot as head chef having learned his craft in Ascot and Stratford. Supported by his second in command Simon Coe and loyal team, Toby has been instrumental in the success of the Cliff Restaurant with unpretentious food with flavour to the fore. Proper food in contemporary surroundings and great local produce, wild sea bass 'hour fresh' from Caldey Island and local Manorbier asparagus still damp from the field are two fine examples.

Pembrokeshire is considered the garden of Wales with its early growing season and its rich, fertile, picturesque countryside that provides a valuable resource reflected in Toby's menus daily.

The Gallery menu, with a panoramic view of Carmarthen Bay is available all day, with the Cliff Restaurant a popular choice for residents and loyal locals for dinner or a traditional Sunday roast. Daily afternoon teas are a must with a special glass of crisp, chilled Champagne. To complement the food, Christophe and his restaurant team entice you to savour and enjoy their fine cellar with a balance of Old and New World wines, offering a warm welcome and unfussy professional service.

Stunning sunsets and large balconies offer unique daytime alfresco relaxation with seasonal cocktails or that favourite nightcap before retiring to one of the hotel's best sea view rooms and serenaded by the sound of the sea.

Relish Restaurant Rewards
See page 007 for details.

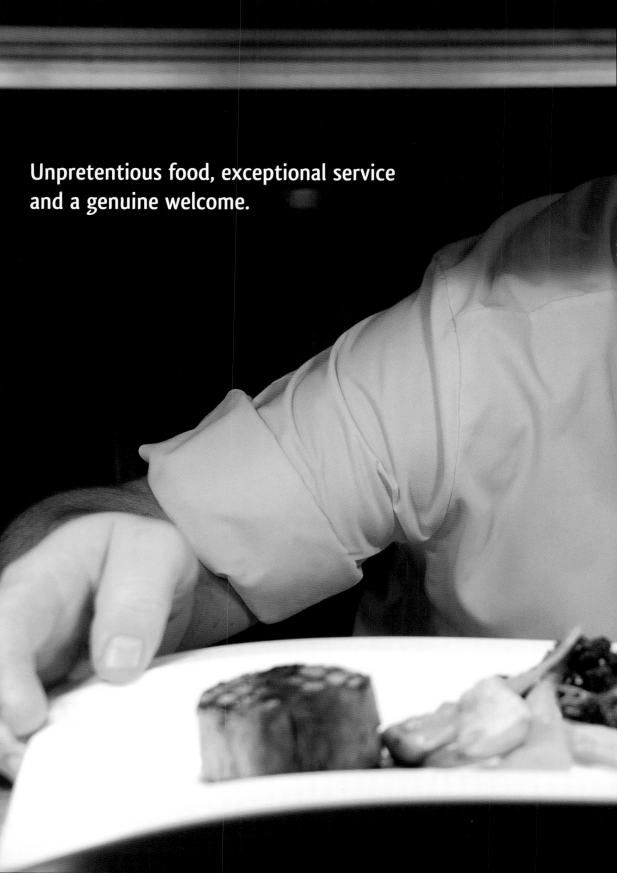

Unpretentious food, exceptional service
and a genuine welcome.

TRIO OF SALMON

SERVES 4

 Un-Oaked Chardonnay Metallico 2011 (California)

Ingredients

Beetroot Marinated Salmon

½ side fresh salmon (skinned, boned)
30g sea salt
100g long life beetroot (grated)
15g granulated sugar
pinch pepper
1 lemon (juice, zest)
15g rosemary (chopped)
1 clove garlic (crushed)

Roulade

300g smoked salmon
100g cream cheese
½ bunch dill (chopped)
½ lemon (juice, zest)

200g hot smoked salmon (cut into nuggets)

Garnish

lemon aioli
watercress
Keta caviar

Method

For The Beetroot Marinated Salmon (Prepare The Day Before)

Combine the ingredients for the marinade. Spread the marinade onto the fresh salmon. Wrap in silicone paper and then in foil. Press lightly and set aside in the fridge overnight.

Remove from the marinade and slice thinly.

For The Roulade (Prepare The Day Before)

Mix the seasonings with the cream cheese. Lay the thinly sliced smoked salmon in a square on some cling film. Smear the cream cheese mix onto the smoked salmon then roll the salmon to form a cylinder shape. Set in the fridge overnight. Slice into portions.

To Serve

Arrange the marinated salmon, a slice of roulade and the hot smoked salmon on plates and garnish with lemon aioli, watercress and Keta caviar.

Chef's Tip

Gently warm the hot smoked salmon to open the texture and flavour. Simply place the salmon on a plate with a teaspoon of sherry, cover with cling film and microwave for 15 seconds.

MEDALLION OF WELSH BEEF FILLET, STEAK & KIDNEY SUET PUDDING, ROASTED PARSNIPS

SERVES 4

 Marques de Ulia Reserva Rioja 2007
(Spain)

Ingredients

Suet Pastry
100g beef suet
200g plain flour
pinch salt
10g baking powder
125ml water

Steak And Kidney
500g diced beef knuckle
200g ox kidney
1 onion (diced)
3 sticks celery (diced)
6 cloves garlic (finely sliced)
500ml stout
1 litre beef stock
salt, pepper, sugar (to season)
cornflour (to thicken)

3 parsnips (peeled, quartered, core removed)
40g salted butter

4 x 125-150g beef fillets

4 x 200ml pudding basins (greased with butter)

Method

For The Suet Pastry
Combine the dry ingredients. Add the water and mix lightly to a firm paste. Leave to rest for 1 hour.

For The Steak And Kidney
Seal the meat and vegetables in a hot pan then remove. *Deglaze* the pan with the stout. Return the meat and vegetables to the pan and gently simmer with the beef stock for 2 hours until the meat is tender. If necessary, add cornflour mixed with a little water to thicken the gravy.

To Make The Puddings
Roll out the pastry to 2½-3mm thickness. Line the buttered basins with the suet pastry. Fill with the steak and kidney mix, reserving some of the gravy for plating. Top with suet pastry lids. Wrap well with cling film. Steam for 45 minutes to 1 hour.

> **Chef's Tip**
> Use disposable foil cups for the suet puddings for ease.

For The Parsnips
Preheat the oven to 185°C (fan).
Combine the butter and parsnips and roast for 20 minutes.

To Assemble The Dish
Seal the beef fillets. Cook rare and rest in a warm place. Plate the dish as shown in the photograph.

COFFEE MOUSSE, COCOA FROTH, PISTACHIO & WHITE CHOCOLATE TRUFFLES

SERVES 4

 Muscat de Rivesaltes 2012
(France)

Ingredients

Truffles
200g white chocolate
40ml double cream
pistachio paste (to taste)
coffee beans (to decorate)

Coffee Mousse
250ml double cream
3 eggs (yolks and whites separated)
75g sugar
2 leaves gelatine
1 shot Kahlua
1 shot espresso

Froth
50ml milk
10g sugar
10g cocoa

Garnish
cocoa powder (to dust)

4 coffee cups

Method

For The Truffles (Prepare The Day Before)

Melt the chocolate over a *bain-marie*. Stir in the cream and pistachio paste. Leave to set in the fridge overnight. Roll into balls, decorate with a coffee bean and set aside.

For The Coffee Mousse

Softly whip the cream and reserve. Whip the egg whites with 25g of sugar and reserve. Whip the yolks with 50g sugar. Melt the gelatine in the Kahlua, then add to the light, fluffy yolks. Add in the whipped cream and combine well. Pour in the espresso shot then fold in the egg whites.

Set the mousse in the serving cups and refrigerate for at least 6 hours.

For The Froth

When you are ready to serve, warm the ingredients together and whisk vigorously. Spoon the bubbles onto the mousse and serve immediately with the truffles and a dusting of cocoa powder.

Chef's Tip
To achieve the best froth, don't overheat the milk.

060
THE CROWN
AT WHITEBROOK

Whitebrook, Near Monmouth, Monmouthshire, NP25 4TX

01600 860 254
www.crownatwhitebrook.co.uk Twitter: @crownwhitebrook

Chris Harrod always had an ambition to be a chef from the age of seven.

From family holidays travelling Britain and Europe staying in restaurants with rooms, a vision was born. It would be located in the countryside and surrounded by immaculate gardens in which he would grow his own produce.

His dreams started to take shape when he worked alongside Raymond Blanc at Le Manoir aux Quat'Saisons.

At the Crown he went one better. The idyllic restaurant with rooms is located in the heart of the Wye valley. A stream meanders through the adjacent valley, forests rise all around, goats graze in fields and deer amble past the door.

"Our location gives the restaurant its identity," says Chris, "our dishes are rooted in French gastronomy. We are inspired by the most amazing local ingredients, foraged herbs and mushrooms from the valley."

Chris continues to move his food forward building on the recognition that he already achieved at Colette's restaurant, achieving 3 AA Rosettes. Visit Wales and The AA both grade The Crown as a 5 star restaurant with rooms.

Restaurant manager Steve Mason has followed Chris' vision for the restaurant by creating a wine list championing local and English wines, independent growers, organic and biodynamic producers and lesser-known grape varieties.

The Crown has eight individually decorated rooms, a place to rest your head and experience the peace and tranquillity the valley has to offer.

Relish Restaurant Rewards
See page 007 for details.

Here at The Crown at Whitebrook we believe that flavours and produce outweigh the formalities of traditional restaurant service. We aim to ensure all our guests have a relaxing and memorable dining experience.

ROAST JERUSALEM ARTICHOKES, GOAT'S CURD, NUTS & SEEDS, ROSEMARY EMULSION

SERVES 4

 Tomero Torrontes, 2011, Mendoza (Argentina)

Ingredients

Artichokes
20 medium sized Jerusalem artichokes (washed, peeled, halved. Reserve the peelings for crisps)
50ml groundnut oil
25g unsalted butter
salt and freshly ground pepper

120g local goat's curd

Rosemary *Emulsion*
200ml milk
2 sprigs rosemary
2g lecithin
salt

Nuts And Seeds
30g pine nuts
30g pumpkin seeds
30g sunflower seeds

Garnish
125g Wye Valley ewe's milk cheese (shaved)
foraged herbs, cresses and mushrooms
artichoke crisps

Method

For The Seeds
Toast the pine nuts, pumpkin and sunflower seeds by putting them in a dry frying pan over a medium heat and gently cooking until golden.

For The Rosemary *Emulsion*
Heat the milk in a small saucepan with 2 sprigs of rosemary. Infuse for 15 minutes over a low heat. Remove the rosemary and add the lecithin powder. Mix with a hand blender for about 1 minute until frothy.

For The Jerusalem Artichokes
Preheat the oven to 180°C (fan).

Heat the groundnut oil in an ovenproof pan until hot. Add the artichokes and toss for 2 minutes. Add the butter, then roast in the oven for 35 minutes, turning occasionally. Once cooked, the artichokes will be a rich caramel colour on the outside and have a moist, squishy interior. Season to taste. Keep warm until serving.

For The Artichoke Crisps
Heat your fryer or oil to 170°C. Add the reserved peelings and cook until golden. Strain on paper, lightly season and set aside.

To Serve
Divide the goat's curd in the middle of each plate then spread it out. Sprinkle with the seeds before arranging the artichokes on top. Reheat the rosemary *emulsion* and mix with a hand blender until frothy, then spoon over the artichokes. Garnish the dish with cheese shavings and artichoke crisps. At the restaurant we finish with foraged herbs and mushrooms.

> **Chef's Tip**
> Try to source a local goat's curd, if you can.

SUCKLING PIG WITH CELERIAC, PEAR & SORREL

SERVES 4

🍷 *Vin de Corse, Clos Culombu Rouge, Etienne Suzzoni, 2012 (Corsica)*

Ingredients

Pork Best End

1 x 400g best end of suckling pig (prepared)
30ml groundnut oil
salt and freshly ground pepper

Pork Shoulder

1 shoulder suckling pig
2 tbsp groundnut oil (for frying)
250g course sea salt, blitzed with: 2 cloves garlic, 4 sprigs thyme, 1 sprig rosemary, 1 small bay leaf

Pork Sauce

1kg pork bones and trimmings (chopped)
30ml groundnut oil
135ml dry white wine (reduced by half)
600ml good quality chicken stock
150g button mushrooms (sliced, caramelised)

Celeriac Purée

olive oil (for frying)
600g celeriac (peeled and diced)
salt
50g milk
90g unsalted butter

Celeriac Pear Gratin

350ml whipping cream
1 sprig thyme
½ bay leaf
1 clove garlic
salt, 3 black peppercorns (crushed)
300g potato (peeled, thinly sliced)
300g celeriac (peeled, thinly sliced)
2 pears (peeled, thinly sliced)

To Serve

100g roast diced celeriac
100g roast crosnes (Chinese artichoke)
pear (thinly sliced)
wood sorrel

Method

For The Pork Best End

Preheat the oven to 180°C (fan).

In a hot roasting pan, sear the pork all over in groundnut oil to colour lightly. Season with salt and pepper. Roast for about 25 minutes. Rest for 15 minutes. Slice into cutlets.

For The Pork Shoulder (Start the day before)

Marinate the pork in aromatic salt for 12 hours.

Preheat the oven to 200°C (fan).

Wash off the aromatic salt, place in a roasting tray in the oven for 30 minutes. Reduce to 110°C and continue to cook for 4 hours. When cooked, find the bone and carefully remove. Portion into 4 pieces. Place in a hot frying pan with groundnut oil, skin side down, and cook until crispy.

For The Pork Sauce

In a hot pan, sear the pork bones and trimmings to colour lightly. Discard fat, then *deglaze* with the wine. Add the stock and mushrooms. Bring to the boil and simmer for 20 minutes. Strain and reduce to sauce consistency. Season to taste.

For The Celeriac Purée

Heat a non-stick pan with a little oil, add the chopped celeriac, season with a pinch of salt and gently fry for 45 minutes or until soft and golden brown. Place the celeriac, milk and butter into a food processor and blend until smooth. Pass through a sieve.

For The Celeriac Pear Gratin

Preheat the oven to 170°C (fan).

Boil the cream with the herbs, salt, peppercorns and garlic for 3 minutes. Arrange and overlap the sliced potato, celeriac and pear in a gratin dish. Strain the cream over and press down. Bake for 30 minutes.

To Serve

Place a generous spoonful of celeriac purée on each plate with a piece of each cut of pig. Arrange the vegetables around the pork, spoon over some sauce and garnish with thinly sliced pear and sorrel leaves.

> **Chef's Tip**
> Saddle, leg or shoulder of suckling pig can all be prepared in the same way.

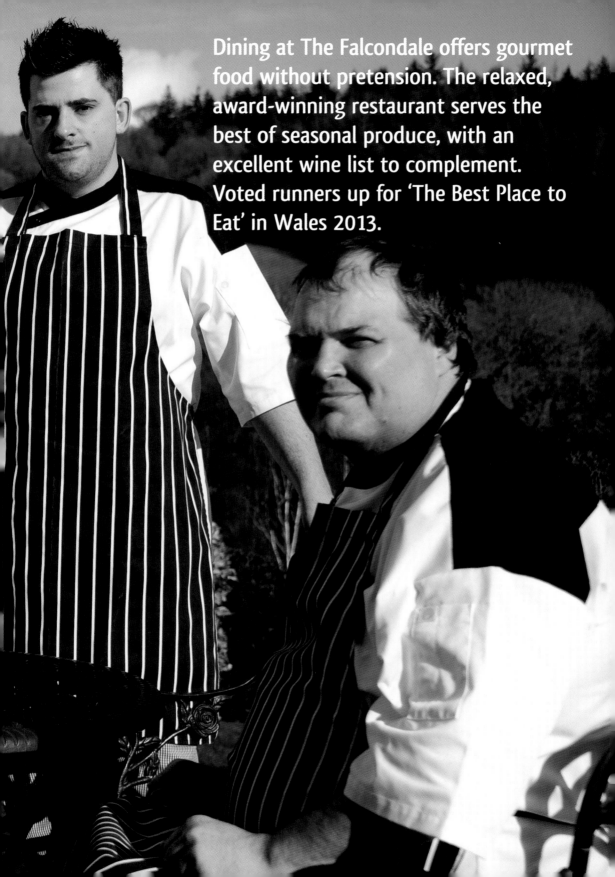

Dining at The Falcondale offers gourmet food without pretension. The relaxed, award-winning restaurant serves the best of seasonal produce, with an excellent wine list to complement. Voted runners up for 'The Best Place to Eat' in Wales 2013.

HAM & EGGS

SERVES 4

 *Pinot Grigio Dolomiti 2012, Alois Lageder,
Alto Adige (Italy)*

Ingredients

Ham Terrine
2 ham hocks
4 litres water
2 bay leaves
7 peppercorns
2 tbsp Dijon mustard
small bunch of parsley (washed, chopped)

Crisp Eggs
4 eggs (softly poached)
2 eggs (beaten)
Panko breadcrumbs (to cover)
2 tbsp plain flour
oil (for deep frying)

Mustard Foam
2 tbsp Dijon mustard
250ml single cream
250ml milk

Garnish
micro herbs
chilli jam

terrine mould 20cm x 10cm lined with cling film

Method

To Prepare The Ham Terrine (Prepare The Day Before)

Simmer the ham hocks in the water with the bay leaves and peppercorns for 3 hours until the ham is falling off the bone. While still warm, remove the hocks and reduce the liquid to a quarter of its original amount.

Pick the ham off the bone removing all bones and sinew. Add the parsley and mustard to the ham, stirring thoroughly. When the liquor has cooled, add to the ham and mix well. Press overnight in a terrine mould in the fridge.

For The Crisp Eggs

Dust the poached eggs in the flour, then roll in the beaten egg and finally the breadcrumbs. Carefully deep fry at 160°C for 1 minute.

To Make The Mustard Foam

Blend the cream, milk and mustard together well before passing through a fine sieve. Pour into a cream whipper and charge when required.

To Serve

Slice the terrine into portions and serve as pictured.

> **Chef's Tip**
> A whipper is not found in many home kitchens, so why not serve with piccalilli instead?

RED MULLET WITH CLAM & MUSSEL BROTH

SERVES 4

🍷 *Rully 2008, Jean-Claude Boisset, Nuits-St-Georges (Burgundy, France)*

Ingredients

4 fillets red mullet
1 tbsp oil (for frying)

Braised Fennel

2 fennel bulbs (thinly sliced)
50g butter
560ml fish stock (hot)

Crushed New Potatoes

200g new potatoes
2 tbsp olive oil
bunch of chives (chopped)
1 clove garlic (crushed)

Broth

2 shallots (finely diced)
50g butter
24 clams (cleaned)
24 mussels (cleaned, debearded)
30ml white wine
300ml fish stock
2 tbsp parsley (chopped)

Method

For The Braised Fennel

Preheat a fan oven to 180ºC. *Sauté* the fennel in the butter in an ovenproof pan until it starts to soften, before adding the fish stock. Bake in the oven for 15 minutes.

For The Crushed New Potatoes

Boil the new potatoes in salted water until soft. When still warm, crush with a fork then add to a frying pan with the oil, chives and garlic until they start to colour.

To Make The Broth

Sweat the shallots in the butter until soft in a large stock pan, before adding the clams and mussels. Add white wine and reduce a little, then add the fish stock, cover with a lid and reduce again for 2-3 minutes. Discard any shells that have not opened. Finally, add the parsley.

When You Are Ready To Serve

Once the above elements are ready, pan fry the mullet fillets until the flesh is translucent and serve in a bowl.

Chef's Tip
To get a crispy skin on the fish, cook three quarters of the way with the skin side down before turning.

WHITE CHOCOLATE & GREEN TEA MOUSSE WITH LEMONGRASS & LIME SORBET

SERVES 4

Plantagenet Ringbark Riesling 2009, Great Southern (Australia)

Ingredients

Mousse

2 tbsp green tea
350ml double cream
250g white chocolate
8 egg yolks
110g caster sugar
7 bronze gelatine leaves

Sorbet

2 stalks lemongrass
2 limes (juice and zest of)
600g sugar
1 litre water

Chocolate Case

100g of 75% solid dark chocolate
10cm x 5cm sheet acetate

Clear Shard

20g isomalt powder

Garnish

edible flowers
few dots lemon curd
1 digestive biscuit (crumbed)

Method

For The Mousse

Place the green tea and cream in a pan and gently simmer. Melt the chocolate in a bowl on a pan of simmering water (*bain-marie*). Whisk the egg yolks and sugar together until pale. Combine the infused cream and eggs together before adding the melted chocolate. Soak the gelatine as per packet instructions. Add the soaked gelatine to the chocolate mousse mixture and combine thoroughly. Pour the mixture in a container of your choice and chill for at least 2 hours.

To Make The Sorbet

Place all the ingredients into a saucepan and bring to the boil. Remove from the heat and leave to stand for 30 minutes, allowing the flavours to infuse. Strain the mixture and, once cool, churn in an ice cream machine until set.

> **Chef's Tip**
> The sorbet can be placed in a container in the freezer and stirred every 30 minutes until completely frozen.

To Make The Chocolate Case

Melt the chocolate and pipe it onto the acetate into a decorative pattern. Bring the ends of the acetate together (to make a cylinder shape) and tape. Set in the fridge. When ready to serve, peel off the acetate.

To Make The Clear Shard

Place the isomalt powder on a tray and into a preheated oven at 180°C for 20 minutes.

The powder will melt and form a clear sheet. Remove from the oven and set aside on a cool surface to harden. Snap into desired shapes.

To Serve

Serve as pictured.

080
THE GROVE

Molleston, Narberth, Pembrokeshire, SA67 8BX

01834 860915
www.thegrove-narberth.co.uk Twitter: @GroveNarberth

Nestling in the heart of the beautiful Pembrokeshire countryside, The Grove is one of Wales' finest restaurants and a leading, small, luxury hotel. It is set within beautifully manicured lawns, flower borders, meadows and mature trees - and a region that offers a great selection of delicious ingredients. The Grove is today renowned as one of the country's most unique, privately owned venues. Its head chef, Duncan Barham, designs his delicious lunch and dinner menus using the finest meats and vegetables of the season.

Duncan's food has won national awards and critical acclaim, including 3 AA Rosettes, Wales Tourism Awards for Best Place to Eat in Wales in 2011 and a listing in the Good Food Guide where the cooking score is currently '5'. Duncan has an extremely talented brigade of eight chefs, some of whom have been with him now for over three years.

The restaurant serves modern British food using locally sourced ingredients that are as fresh as possible, much of which come from The Grove's extensive kitchen gardens.

The Grove offers a truly intimate and sumptuous dining experience with warming log fires throughout the house. The restaurant is surrounded by trees, gardens and wildflower meadows to provide a magnificent setting whatever the time of year. The terrace is also perfect for enjoying al fresco eating throughout the summer months.

Apart from food, The Grove offers 20 intimate guest rooms and suites, together with four traditional cottages that are full of character - with interiors individually designed to the highest standards.

Gaze out of the windows for scenic views of the Preseli mountains, or make the short trip to Pembrokeshire National Park for stunning country walks.

Relish Restaurant Rewards
See page 007 for details.

Go to enjoy great food, fine wines and a wee bit of luxury in this most stunning part of Wales soon.

90
HANSON AT THE CHELSEA

17 St Mary Street, Swansea, SA1 3LH

T: 01792 464 068
www.hansonatthechelsea.co.uk

t's no wonder Andrew Hanson runs a market menu at his restaurant, near the heart of Swansea city centre.

The acclaimed chef is just a stone's throw from the bustling Swansea Market, which means he has the pick of the finest produce in South Wales.

"The market is just across the road from us," says the 2 AA Rosette chef. "We're in there all the time. We've got great produce and plenty of choice - how many other restaurants can walk out of their door and take their pick from three different fishmongers?"

Having trained in the Ritz Hotel London, Andrew ventured back to Swansea, where his reputation now preceeds him.

Andrew Hanson has been cooking at Hanson at The Chelsea for eight years and has made a huge success of the restaurant he runs alongside his wife, Michelle.

"We have incredible fish," Andrew adds. "I used to watch the trawlers and go down to the harbour; the fishermen would keep the best boxes back just for me. The fishmongers do just the same these days, at the market."

Andrew Hanson at The Chelsea serves clean, natural flavours that reflect the seasons.

"I won't cook things that are out of season," says Andrew. "The food has to be sustainable. I won't take female fish if it's full of roe, it ought to be left in the sea to produce the next generation."

Andrew has built on his wealth of restaurant experiences to offer the customers at Hanson's a menu that's full of big flavours and classic combinations. "We treat exceptional ingredients with the utmost respect," says Andrew.

"That's why we have such a loyal clientele as we combine a gourmet menu of fine food with just the right balance of friendly, personal service."

Relish Restaurant Rewards
See page 007 for details.

Recently voted as one of The Times top 10 fish restaurants in the UK, with 2 AA Rosettes and also an award for best value restaurant in Wales, Hanson at The Chelsea Restaurant will not disappoint.

CRUMBED FREE RANGE GOWER DUCK EGG, BLACK PUDDING, CRACKLING, BACON, ASPARAGUS & HOLLANDAISE SAUCE

SERVES 4

 *Marlborough Sauvignon Blanc
(New Zealand)*

Ingredients

4 slices black pudding
4 pieces smoked, streaky bacon
4 muffins (toasted, buttered)

Crackling

24cm piece pig skin
salt

Hollandaise Sauce

125g butter
2 egg yolks
½ tsp white wine vinegar
salt (pinch of)
lemon juice (optional)

Crumbed Duck Eggs

4 free range duck eggs (room temperature)
flour (to coat)
1 egg (beaten, to egg wash)
50g breadcrumbs (to coat)

Asparagus

16 asparagus stems
25g butter (melted)

To Garnish

mixed leaves
truffle oil
balsamic glaze (to dress plate)

Method

For The Crackling

Preheat the oven to 220°C.

Dry the pig skin thoroughly and remove any hairs. Salt generously, then place in the oven for 40-50 minutes until crispy and the skin starts to bubble. Cut into 4 portions when still warm.

For The Hollandaise Sauce

In a pan, slowly melt the butter and skim off any impurities. Whisk the egg yolks with the vinegar and salt until pale in colour and it's beginning to thicken. Place the bowl over a *bain-marie* and slowly add the melted butter, whisking constantly. If it appears too thick, add a little water or lemon juice to thin down. Keep warm until required.

For The Crumbed Duck Eggs

Simmer the eggs for 5 minutes, peel and leave to cool. Once cool, dip into the flour, followed by the egg wash, and finally the breadcrumbs. When nearly ready to serve, deep fry at 160°C until golden.

For The Asparagus

Blanch the asparagus in boiling water, drain, then roll in the melted butter.

To Serve

Toast the muffins and butter them. Grill the bacon under a hot grill, cook the black pudding in a hot, dry pan and arrange on the muffin with the crackling. Lay the asparagus on the plate, then add the hollandaise sauce. Put the crumbed egg on top of the black pudding and cut it in half. Dress the mixed leaves with truffle oil and garnish the plate with balsamic glaze.

Chef's Tip

Always try to secure the freshest eggs possible for the breaded eggs and the hollandaise sauce.

WILD GOWER SEA BASS WITH SWANSEA MARKET SEAFOOD, BUTTER & HERB SAUCE

SERVES 4

 Gavi di Gavi, Quinta Do Noval (Italy)

Ingredients

4 wild bass fillets (seasoned)
oil (for frying)
800g assorted clams, mussels, Dublin Bay prawns, scallops, shell on prawns, live cockles (or any seafood of your choice)
50g butter
4 shallots (finely chopped)
150ml dry white wine
salt and pepper
handful parsley, dill, chervil (chopped)

Method

For The Seafood With Butter And Herb Sauce

In a large *sauté* pan, melt a knob of the butter with the shallots and allow to soften. Add the mixed seafood (except the live cockles as they open very quickly). When the seafood is almost cooked through, 2-3 minutes, add the cockles and herbs.
Add the wine and seasoning, shake the pan then drain off some liquid. Stir in the remainder of the butter. Keep warm.

Chef's Tip
Keep your herbs in ice chilled water to keep them fresh and full of colour.

For The Sea Bass

Heat a little oil in a pan and add the sea bass fillets, skin side down. Cook for 2-3 minutes until the fish looks as though it has cooked two thirds of the way through and the skin is crispy. Turn the fish over and cook for a further minute. Take care not to overcook the fillets.

To Serve

Arrange the mixed seafood on a plate with sea bass on top. Drizzle with the herb butter sauce.

The restaurant is situated in the original building dating back to 1811 that was the harbourmaster's office. Overlooking the fishing boats, it's a relaxed space that serves the freshest of foods. A winner of Wales the True Taste awards, it has been featured in the Good Food Guide every year since opening. Ludo was a semi-finalist in Professional Master Chef in 2009 and is a recognised figure within Welsh food circles.

HARBOURMASTER CARLINGFORD OYSTER PLATTER

SERVES 4

 Muscadet Côtes de Grandlieu Sur Lie, 'Le Demi-Boeuf' Vignoble Malidain (France)

Ingredients

Carlingford Oysters

24 Carlingford oysters (shucked carefully to retain the juice)

Muscadet White Wine Oyster Jelly

1½ leaves gelatine
250ml Muscadet white wine
1 small shallot (finely diced)
1 tbsp fresh chives (finely chopped)

Oysters With Cucumber Spaghetti And Horseradish Cream

1 cucumber (cut in half lengthways, de-seeded)
200ml whipping cream
2 tbsp fresh horseradish (grated)
salt and white pepper (to season)

Apple, Ginger And Lime Oyster

1 Granny Smith apple
½ lime (juice of)
1 tsp freshly grated ginger

Method

For The White Wine Oyster Jelly

Carefully remove the flesh from 8 oysters, reserving the juice.

Soak the gelatine in cold water until soft.

Place the wine in a small saucepan and add the sieved oyster juice and diced shallot. Bring to the boil. Remove from the heat. Stir in the gelatine until dissolved. Add the oyster flesh and allow to cool.

When cold, but not set, add the chives. Sit each oyster back into an empty shell and top each with the jelly mixture. Leave to set in the fridge for 30 minutes before serving.

For The Oyster With Cucumber Spaghetti And Horseradish Cream

Cut the cucumber into long *julienne* strips and freeze.
When completely frozen, remove from the freezer to defrost.

Carefully remove the flesh from another 8 oysters. Lay a few defrosted cucumber 'strings' on a board, place an oyster in the centre and wrap. Repeat the process with the remaining 7 oysters.

Make The Horseradish Cream

Whisk the cream to a hard peak and add the grated horseradish. Mix to combine. Place a teaspoon of cream in the empty oyster shell and carefully sit a cucumber wrapped oyster on top.

Apple, Ginger And Lime Oyster

Loosen the flesh of the remaining 8 oysters from their shells using a small sharp knife.

Combine the lime juice and ginger in a bowl. Slice the apple into *julienne* strips and add to the lime and ginger juice.

Spoon the mixture over the oysters.

To Serve

Arrange the Carlingford oysters on a platter and serve.

> **Chef's Tip**
> Open oysters from the side for ease and to avoid damaging the flesh.

GRILLED CARDIGAN BAY LOBSTER WITH THAI BUTTER, STRAW POTATOES & ASIAN SLAW

SERVES 4

 Man O' War 'Exiled', Ponui Island, Pinot Gris
(New Zealand)

Ingredients

Thai Butter

250g salted butter (softened)
1 bunch fresh coriander (chopped)
3cm piece fresh ginger (peeled, grated)
3 sticks lemongrass (finely chopped)
3 cloves garlic (peeled, crushed)
2 red chillies (finely chopped)
1 tsp tomato purée
2 limes (zest, juice of)

Grilled Cardigan Bay Lobster

2 x 500g live Cardigan Bay lobsters
200g salt

Asian Slaw

2 carrots (peeled, grated)
½ white cabbage (finely sliced)
2 onions (finely chopped)
½ bunch fresh coriander (chopped)
4 sprigs fresh mint (chopped)
2 tsp caster sugar
1 tsp salt
1 red chilli (deseeded, finely chopped)

Straw Potatoes

800g Maris Piper potatoes (peeled)
sunflower oil (for frying)
salt (to season)

you will require a mandolin to make the
straw potatoes

Method

For The Thai Butter

Place the softened butter in a blender or food processor and add the remaining ingredients. Blend until combined.

Transfer the herbed butter mixture to a sheet of cling film and roll into a sausage shape. Twist the ends to secure tightly and chill in the fridge until firm.

For The Cardigan Bay lobster

Place 5 litres of water in a large pan and add the salt. Bring to the boil. Quickly add the lobster, cover and boil for 5 minutes. Remove the lobster from the water and allow to cool enough to handle. Repeat with the second lobster.

Place the lobster on a chopping board and cut in half lengthways using a large, heavy knife. Remove and discard both the sac from behind the eyes and the black intestine that runs the length of the lobster tail.

Crack the claws using the back of the knife. Re-arrange the tails, left to right and right to left.

For The Asian Slaw

Place the ingredients in a large bowl, stir to combine and chill until needed.

To Make The Straw Potatoes

Using a mandolin, cut the potatoes into *julienne* strips and rinse under cold running water to remove the starch. The water should run clean. Transfer to a tea towel and pat dry to remove excess water.

In a large pan, add sunflower oil to a depth of approximately 6-8cm. Heat to 180°C.

Cook the potato strips in small batches until golden brown and crisp. Remove and place on kitchen paper to drain. Continue with the remaining potato strips and sprinkle with salt.

Chef's Tip

Use a thermometer to check the temperature of the oil or alternatively add a small strip of potato. The potato should sizzle immediately. When frying the straw potatoes, do not overcrowd the pan.

To Assemble The Dish

Preheat the grill to a medium heat. Place the lobster halves on the grill tray, flesh side up.

Dot the lobster flesh with pieces of the chilled Thai butter and splash with a little water to moisten.

Grill for approximately 8-10 minutes, basting regularly, until the flesh is firm and lightly golden.

Place half a lobster per person on a serving plate and serve with the straw potatoes and Asian slaw.

PEAR & PERL LAS SOUFFLE

SERVES 4

🍷 *Château du Seuil, Cérons, Semillon, Bordeaux, France*

Ingredients

Soufflé Base
2 ripe Packham pears (peeled, diced)
1 lemon (juice of)
50g caster sugar
4 tbsp water
1 tbsp cornflour
2 tbsp Poire William (pear liqueur)

Meringue
8 egg whites
80g caster sugar (plus extra for ramekins)

Soufflé
50g Perl Las (or other blue cheese)
butter (to grease the ramekins)
icing sugar (to dust)

Garnish
Perl Las (or other blue cheese)
poached pears (sliced)

4 ramekins

Method

For The Soufflé Base
Place the pears in a saucepan with the lemon juice, sugar and water. Simmer over a medium heat for about 5 minutes until soft. Mash with the back of a fork, transfer to a food processor and blend until smooth. In a small bowl, blend the cornflour and Poire William to a smooth paste. Return the puréed pears to the pan. Add the cornflour mixture and whisk until smooth, over a high heat.

To Make The Meringue
Preheat the oven to 190°C.

Before you begin to whisk the egg whites, prepare the ramekins for the soufflé.

Lightly butter 4 ramekins. Coat the inside of the ramekins with caster sugar, tipping out any excess.

in a large, grease-free bowl, whisk the egg whites until frothy. Add the sugar and whisk until firm.

To Make The Soufflé
Mix one third of the meringue mixture with the soufflé base until smooth. Lightly fold in the remaining meringue using a metal spoon. Half fill the ramekins with the mixture then add some crumbled Perl Las. Top with the rest of the mixture. Smooth the surface with a palette knife.

Place in the preheated oven for 7-8 minutes.

Dust with icing sugar and serve immediately.

Chef's Tip
Run a thumb nail around the inside rim of the ramekins. This helps the soufflés rise evenly without catching on the sides.

110
THE HARDWICK

Old Raglan Road, Abergavenny, Monmouthshire, NP7 9AA

01873 854 220
www.thehardwick.co.uk Twitter: @_thehardwick

Under the tutelage of head chef Stephen Terry, The Hardwick has become one of the UK's most sought after restaurants.

It has won the Welsh Restaurant of the Year for two successive years - a title well deserved thanks to exceptional food and friendly, informal service.

The flavours at The Hardwick are robust and make the best of local, seasonal ingredients. Classy dishes showcase exceptional local meat, sublime Welsh fruit and vegetables and fish caught from the nation's shoreline.

Terry has a reputation for excellence. He served his apprenticeship under Marco Pierre White and Michel Roux Jr at Harvey's and Le Gavroche. He earned his first Michelin star at the age of 25 and after making a number of stops at illustrious venues, including The Walnut Tree, he arrived at The Hardwick in 2005.

"We are in a beautiful part of the world with great producers right on our doorstep. Our food is a celebration of this area."

Terry has helped to transform the venue and has a reputation for food that explodes with flavour and is deliciously unfussy.

The Hardwick, however, is about more than just the food. Service is with a smile and the venue's three separate dining rooms exude character.

Natural woods, artworks from local artists and vintage furnishings make it undeniably comfortable and welcoming. Jazzy sounds help to create a vibrant atmosphere and food made by local producers is showcased on Terry's bar.

"Welsh food has experienced a renaissance in recent years," adds Terry. "Our national cuisine is seriously exciting and we're proud to be a part of it."

Relish Restaurant Rewards
See page 007 for details.

At the Hardwick the choice is almost ridiculous for the size of the restaurant. This doesn't make for an easy life but it works and customers enjoy visiting for old favourites and new dishes alike.

CONFIT DUCK HASH WITH CHICORY & BLOOD ORANGE

SERVES 4

 Chenin Blanc Reserva, Ken Forrester Stellenbosch (South Africa)

Ingredients

Confit Duck Hash

2 large duck legs
250g duck fat
1 large white onion (peeled, finely sliced)
1 large Maris Piper potato (peeled, cut into 1½cm dice)
4 duck eggs
Tabasco
Worcestershire sauce
salt
200ml brown chicken stock (reduced by half)

Garnish

1 large head chicory (cut lengthways into 4)
25g caster sugar
2 blood oranges (peeled, segmented, reserve juice from the carcass)
100ml orange juice
100ml olive oil
seasonal leaves

4 x 8cm rings

Method

For The *Confit* Duck Hash (Prepare In Advance)

Preheat the oven to 110°C (fan).

Place the duck legs in a roasting dish, cover with the duck fat, a piece of parchment paper and tin foil the dish. Place in the oven for 6 hours. Allow to cool in the duck fat to room temperature. Remove legs from the fat and drain.

Preheat the oven to 170°C (fan).

Carefully remove the skin from the duck legs and transfer the skin to a non-stick baking tray.

Roast in the oven for 7-9 minutes to crisp up the skin. Remove and allow to cool. Carefully remove the duck meat from the bone, place into a bowl and leave to one side.

Caramelise the sliced onions in a tablespoon of duck fat. Cook the diced potato in salted water until they drop off the end of a knife. Drain and cool then deep fry until golden brown.

For The Garnish

Make a dry caramel with the caster sugar in a small pan and add the orange juices to the caramel, then reduce by two thirds. Remove from the heat, allow to cool and whisk in the olive oil to make the dressing.

Place the chicory quarters in a hot pan with a splash of olive oil and colour on all sides. Remove and marinate with the orange flavoured dressing.

To Serve

Bring the reduced chicken stock to the boil in a small frying pan, add the caramelised onions and reduce the heat by half.
To make the hash, add the *confit* duck, crispy duck skin, fried potatoes and season to taste with salt, Worcestershire sauce and Tabasco.

Fry 4 duck eggs in duck fat being careful not to overcook the yolks, as their runniness is integral to the dish.

Divide the hash into 4 and place into a ring on each plate, pressing down to create a neat duck puck. Using the same ring, cut the duck egg out and place on top. Garnish the plates with marinated chicory, blood orange segments, seasonal leaves and dressing.

Chef's Tip
Don't overcook the duck egg yolk!

ROAST RUMP & BRAISED SHOULDER OF BRECON LAMB WITH BUBBLE & SQUEAK, JERUSALEM ARTICHOKES & SALSA VERDE

SERVES 4

🍷 *Pinot Noir 'The Hounds' 2011, Allan Scott, Marlborough (New Zealand)*

Ingredients

Breaded Lamb Shoulder
1 small lamb shoulder
2 carrots (peeled, cut in half)
2 sticks celery
1 onion (peeled, halved through the root)
4 cloves garlic (unpeeled)
1 sprig rosemary, 1 sprig thyme
plain flour (to dust)
1 egg (beaten), fine breadcrumbs (to coat)

Lamb Rumps
4 x 170g lamb rumps (trimmed, seasoned with salt and pepper)
1 tbsp oil
1 sprig rosemary, 2 cloves garlic
50g butter

Bubble And Squeak
2 large Maris Piper potatoes (washed, peeled, quartered, boiled until soft)
200g cooked Savoy cabbage leaves (roughly chopped)
100ml rapeseed oil, salt and pepper
(braised vegetables from the lamb shoulder)

Salsa Verde
Blitz: 50g tarragon (picked), 50g chives, 50g parsley (picked), 50g mint (picked), olive oil, juices from lamb rumps, add lemon juice to taste

Tapenade
Blitz: 90g pitted black olives, 1 anchovy, 1 tsp Lilliput capers, ½ clove garlic, 50ml olive oil

Artichokes
4 medium Jerusalem artichokes (scrubbed, dried off)
olive oil to coat, salt and pepper

purple sprouting broccoli (steamed)

Method

For The Breaded Lamb Shoulder (Prepare The Day Before)
Preheat the oven to 140°C (fan).

Place the lamb shoulder into a deep oven tray with the vegetables and herbs and add enough water to half cover the shoulder. Cover the lamb with a sheet of greaseproof paper then cover the whole tray with foil. Roast for 4 hours. Remove the lamb and vegetables and reduce the liquid by three quarters, in a pan.

Pull the tender lamb meat from the bone and place into a bowl. Add the reduced stock and mix well, season. Line a suitable sized tray with cling film leaving enough overhanging to cover. Set the meat mixture into it, fold the cling film over the mixture, then place another tray (preferably the same size) to weigh it down and compact the meat. Chill for 4-5 hours.

Once chilled and set firmly, remove the cling film and transfer to a chopping board. Cut into 3cm cube shaped portion sizes. Roll lightly in flour, dip in egg wash then roll in breadcrumbs. Deep fry until golden at 180°C then place in the oven at 180°C (fan) for a few minutes to warm through. Season with salt.

For The Lamb Rumps
Preheat the oven to 180°C (fan).

Heat the oil in an ovenproof pan. Place the rumps in, skin side down, brown them all over and add garlic, rosemary and butter. Place in oven for about 14-16 minutes. Once rested this will be pink. Adjust cooking times to suit your cooking preference. Leave to rest on a small plate before carving and use the juices by adding these to the salsa verde just before serving.

For The Bubble And Squeak
Roughly chop all the drained and reserved braising vegetables from the cooking of the lamb shoulder. Smash the roast potatoes with the back of a fork in a bowl and mix with the braising vegetables and the cooked cabbage leaves.

Pan fry the mixture until lightly golden brown and check the seasoning. Keep hot until serving.

For The Baked, Deep Fried Artichokes
Preheat the oven to 160°C (fan) and roast whole for approximately an hour. Cool then quarter. Deep fry at 180°C until golden and crispy. Drain and season.

To Serve
Plate as pictured and serve with the tapenade, salsa verde and steamed purple sprouting broccoli.

STEM GINGER CHEESECAKE WITH RHUBARB JELLY

SERVES 4

 Moscato d'Asti
(Italy)

Ingredients

Rhubarb Jelly

500g forced rhubarb (washed, trimmed,
cut into ½cm pieces)
100g caster sugar
3 leaves gelatine

Ginger Cheesecake

375g cream cheese
115g caster sugar
15g cornflour
50g stem ginger (puréed)
1 large egg
150ml double cream

Ginger Shortbread Crunch

50g soft butter
75g plain flour
40g stem ginger (puréed)
1 heaped tbsp cornflour
¼ tsp baking powder
½ tsp vanilla extract

4 x 120ml moulds for the jelly
20cm square cake tin for cheesecake

Method

For The Rhubarb Jelly (Prepare The Day Before)

Mix the rhubarb with the sugar and place into a colander, cover and refrigerate overnight. On removing the rhubarb from the fridge you will notice that it has bled and you should have approximately 400g of juice that has drained from the rhubarb.

Warm a quarter of this juice in a pan and melt the gelatine leaves. Add this back to the remaining liquid, place the rhubarb into desired moulds and cover with juice. Leave to set for 4 hours.

For The Ginger Cheesecake

Preheat the oven to 150°C (fan).

Combine the cream cheese, sugar, cornflour and ginger thoroughly. Beat the egg into the mixture, followed by the cream.

Spoon the mixture into a small cake tin lined with greaseproof paper and bake for approximately 20-25 minutes.

When cooked, place into a food processor and blitz until smooth. Pour into a suitable bowl and allow to cool and set in the fridge.

For The Ginger Shortbread Crunch

Preheat the oven to 160°C (fan).

Mix all ingredients thoroughly together and place on a parchment lined tray. Bake for 12-15 minutes or until golden brown. Allow to cool and crumble the ginger shortbread crunch into small bite size pieces. Store in an airtight container until needed.

To Serve

Rocher 2 spoons of cheesecake onto a plate, turn out the jelly and garnish with ginger shortbread crunch.

> **Chef's Tip**
> Although the rhubarb jelly needs to be started the day before you intend to serve this, all elements of this dish may be prepared the day before, to make life a little easier for you.

120
THE INN AT PENALLT

Penallt, Monmouthshire, NP25 4SE

01600 772 765
www.theinnatpenallt.co.uk

From run down pub to award-winning country inn.

Four years ago Jackie and Andrew sold their house and bought a near closed pub just outside of Monmouth. Following a complete refurbishment and having been joined by head chef Peter Hulsmann, the couple opened The Inn at Penallt in March 2010. Since then, The Inn has firmly established itself amongst Monmouth's array of quality restaurants and inns.

The Inn's first AA Rosette was quickly followed by being named AA Pub of the Year for Wales 2012/13 and inclusion in the latest Michelin Guide to Eating Out.

Peter and his team's ethos is simple - source the best local ingredients, take time in the preparation, care in the cooking and let the dishes speak for themselves. The results are classic favourites, with intense depths of flavour and interesting twists. Fresh bread, preserves, chutneys, ice creams and even butter churned from local double cream are made in the kitchen. The food is complemented by a well-chosen selection of fine wines, craft ciders and ales from local artisan producers and brewers.

Out front, the welcome is as warm as the log fire in winter or the stunning views in summer. After all as Jackie said "If I'm going to own an Inn, it has to be one I would like to visit."

Our team is a small family. We all take great pride in serving our guests. Blessed with an abundance of quality local producers our aim has always been to offer the best dishes we can in an attentive, relaxed atmosphere.

Relish Restaurant Rewards
See page 007 for details.

The recognition has been amazing; AA Rosette, AA Pub of the Year for Wales and inclusion in the 2014 Michelin Guide to Eating Out, but by far the most rewarding acknowledgement of all, is our wonderful customers who visit and recommend us.

HOME CURED MUSCOVY DUCK BREAST, WATERCRESS, PEAR & TOASTED PINE NUT SALAD

SERVES 4

 Huia Chardonnay, Marlborough (New Zealand)

Ingredients

The Duck
1 large fresh Muscovy duck breast
50g sea salt
1 tsp crushed black pepper
1 tsp fresh thyme
6 juniper berries (crushed)

The Pear Salad
2 bunches fresh watercress
2 pears
50g pine nuts (toasted)

The Dressing
2 tbsp aged balsamic vinegar
6 tbsp extra virgin olive oil
salt

muslin cloth

Method

For The Duck (Prepare 2 weeks ahead)
Score the duck skin with a sharp knife. Combine the remaining ingredients and massage them into the duck breast. Place in a small, airtight, plastic container in the fridge for 24 hours. Wash off with cold water, dry, wrap in the muslin cloth and leave in the fridge for 12 days.

For The Pear Salad
Wash the watercress, shake well and pat dry. Peel the pears then cut lengthways into 4 even quarters. Heat a heavy bottomed frying pan until almost smoking. Add the pine nuts, moving the pan constantly on the heat to toss the nuts until light brown, for about 30-60 seconds. Tip nuts onto a plate to cool.

For The Dressing
Combine the balsamic vinegar and olive oil. Season with a pinch of salt.

To Serve
Carve the duck breast into paper thin slices. Toss the watercress in the dressing. Arrange on the plate, then add the pear, sliced duck breast and pine nuts as pictured. Finish with a grind of black pepper.

Chef's Tip
If you don't have a meat slicer for the duck breast, use a very sharp, long bladed ham knife and cut horizontally.

SADDLE OF BRECON VENISON, QUINCE JELLY & VENISON SAUCE, POTATO CROQUETTE

SERVES 4

 St Cosme Côtes du Rhône
(France)

Ingredients

Venison And Black Pudding
1 x 800g saddle of venison (rubbed with
oil, seasoned)
3 tbsp rapeseed oil
4 slices black pudding (1cm thick)
salt and pepper

The Stock
2kg venison bones
4 tbsp rapeseed oil
1 large onion (roughly sliced)
1 leek (roughly sliced)
4 sticks celery (roughly sliced)
2 carrots (roughly sliced)
6 peppercorns, 12 juniper berries
2 dsp tomato purée
2 bay leaves
enough water to cover all stock ingredients

Quince Jelly And Venison Sauce
2 tbsp quince jelly
500ml venison stock, 1 tsp butter

Apple Crisps
1 green apple (thinly sliced)
1 dsp caster sugar, ½ lemon (juice of)

Sweet And Sour Braised Red Cabbage
1 red cabbage (shredded)
2 medium onions (shredded)
500ml cooking red wine, 250ml vinegar
300-350g sugar
2 large cooking apples (peeled, sliced)

For The Potato Croquettes
600g floury potatoes (boiled until soft, drained)
3-4 egg yolks
¼ onion (finely chopped)
50g smoked streaky bacon (finely diced)
pinch nutmeg
salt and pepper (to season)
flour, 1 egg, breadcrumbs (all to coat)

Method

For The Venison Stock
Heat the rapeseed oil in a large, heavy saucepan, add bones and toss for 2-3 minutes until brown. In a separate pan, heat a little more oil and fry the sliced vegetables for 2-4 minutes until brown. Add remaining dry ingredients, cook for another 2 minutes, then transfer to the pan with the venison bones. Cover with water, bring to the boil, simmer for 2-3 hours. Strain through muslin, remove excess fat, put back in pan and reduce to approximately 500ml.

For The Venison
Preheat the oven to 220°C.
Heat 2 tablespoons of oil in a pan, seal the venison, then place in the oven for 7-8 minutes. Leave in a warm dish for 3-4 minutes to rest.

For The Black Pudding
Fry black pudding for 1 minute on each side.

For The Quince Jelly And Venison Sauce
Put the stock into a small saucepan, bring to just off the boil, add the quince jelly and stir until dissolved. Reduce heat to a simmer and gently cook until the sauce thickens. Stir in the butter.

For The Apple Crisps
Preheat the oven to 90°C.
Put the apple on a tray with baking parchment. Dissolve the sugar in the lemon juice and brush the apple slices. Bake for about 2 hours until crisp.

For The Braised Red Cabbage
Place the cabbage and onion in a large saucepan, add sugar, wine and vinegar, cover and cook on a low heat for about 4 hours. Add the apples and cook for a further 30-40 minutes until most of the liquid has reduced.

For The Croquettes
Pass potatoes through a ricer into a mixing bowl, add egg yolks one by one, the nutmeg, salt and pepper. Combine well. Soften the bacon and onion in a pan, drain, add to potato mix, leave to cool. Once cool, shape mixture, coat with flour, egg and breadcrumbs. Deep fry at 160°C for 1-2 minutes or shallow fry until golden.

To Serve
Serve as pictured.

> **Chef's Tip**
> Stock will keep in a freezer for 3 months. Redcurrant jelly works equally well as quince.

LEMON SCENTED BREAD & BUTTER PUDDING, PENDERYN WHISKY & MARMALADE ICE CREAM, TUILE BISCUIT

SERVES 4

 *Eclat, Botrytis Semillon
(Chile)*

Ingredients

Ice Cream

142ml double cream
142ml full-fat milk
2 egg yolks
60g caster sugar
2 dsp good quality orange marmalade
35ml Penderyn (or whisky of choice)

Tuile Biscuits

25g butter (very soft)
25g icing sugar
25g plain flour
1 egg white (from a small egg)

Bread And Butter Pudding

12 slices medium sliced bread (cut into discs)
70g butter (softened)
2 eggs
4 tbsp Demerara sugar
100g raisins
150ml full-fat milk
150ml double cream
1 vanilla pod (split)
1 lemon (zest of, finely chopped)
2 dsp caster sugar

4 x 9cm ramekins
7½cm pastry cutter

Method

For The Ice Cream

Bring milk and cream to the boil. Combine egg yolks and sugar in a bowl, add the hot milk and cream, and mix well. Return to a clean pan, stirring constantly. Heat until just off the boil. Pass through a fine sieve. Add the marmalade and whisky. Churn in an ice cream machine.

> **Chef's Tip**
> If you do not have an ice cream machine put in freezer until ice crystals start to form, beat well then return to freezer. Repeat 3 or 4 times until smooth.

For The Tuile Biscuit

Preheat the oven to 180°C.

Sieve flour and icing sugar into a bowl, blend with the butter then fold in the egg white, mix well. Spread a thin layer onto baking parchment, place on a baking tray and cook until golden brown, for about 1-2 minutes.

For The Bread And Butter Pudding

Preheat the oven to 160°C.

Spread the bread with butter. Place a disc of bread into the ramekin, sprinkle with brown sugar and raisins. Repeat until level with top of ramekin.

Bring the cream, milk and vanilla pod to the boil. Set aside to infuse.

Combine the eggs, sugar and lemon in a bowl, pass the milk mixture through a sieve into the eggs and whisk gently. Return to a pan on a low heat and stir constantly until before boiling point. Spoon the mixture into the ramekins, leave to rest for 30 minutes, topping up if necessary.

Sprinkle the top of the puddings with a little more Demerara sugar and raisins. Place in a baking tin, fill with water to two thirds of the ramekin height. Bake for 15-20 minutes. Serve immediately.

To Serve

Plate as pictured and enjoy!

130
LLANERCH VINEYARD

Hensol, Vale of Glamorgan, CF72 8GG

01443 222 716
www.llanerch-vineyard.co.uk

Llanerch Vineyard, owned by the Davies family since 2010, is a working Welsh vineyard, established in 1986, located in the heart of picturesque Glamorganshire, only a short distance from the striking coastal countryside and roaming green hills. Whether you are a keen wine connoisseur and want to sample the signature Welsh wines, or are looking for a unique getaway, Llanerch Vineyard hotel has the perfect combination of relaxation and sophistication to help you unwind.

The laid-back, luxurious atmosphere and perfect location, just 20 minutes from Cardiff, makes the restaurant, bistro, boutique vineyard hotel rooms, self guided vineyard tours and cookery classes popular with locals, day trippers and holiday makers alike.

Our head chef, Andrew Hughes, working with his talented team, has built a reputation for excellence in The Cariad Bistro and newly developed Cariad Restaurant, both of which offer stunning panoramic views over the vineyard.

Andrew has a breadth of experience behind him, having worked in 5 star hotels, Rosette restaurants and under Gordon Ramsay and Jason Atherton in the Maze Michelin star restaurant in London.

The Davies family and Andrew share and wish to promote the same ethos, ensuring they source food as locally as possible, directly 'from farm to plate', and being committed to using seasonal ingredients. The bistro provides relaxed, casual, all day dining from the heart of the farmhouse, extending to the terrace on finer days, whereas the restaurant offers a more formal dining experience for afternoon teas and à la carte menus.

Relish Restaurant Rewards
See page 007 for details.

Head chef Andrew Hughes and his brigade passionately create dishes for you to enjoy in either The Cariad Bistro, or The Cariad Restaurant and at events hosted at Llanerch Vineyard.

DUCK BREAST, DUCK BONBONS, DUCK EGGS, BUTTERNUT SQUASH PUREE

SERVES 4

 Royal Tokaji Dry Furmint,
(Hungary)

Ingredients

1 duck (breasts and legs removed, bones reserved)

Duck Bonbons

duck legs (as above)
500ml olive oil
flour (to coat)
1 egg (beaten, to coat)
Panko breadcrumbs (to coat)

Duck Eggs

4 duck eggs
flour (to coat)
1 egg (beaten, to coat)
Panko breadcrumbs (to coat)

Duck *Jus*

1kg duck bones
1 stick celery (roughly chopped)
1 carrot (roughly chopped)
1 onion (roughly chopped)
500ml red wine

Butternut Squash Purée

1 butternut squash (peeled, diced)
butter (knob of)
50ml vegetable stock

Vegetables

200g new potatoes
30g butter
100g peas
4 cep mushrooms (washed)
3 tbsp olive oil

Garnish

edible flowers

Method

Chef's Tip
Prepare all elements before cooking the duck breast.

For The Duck Bonbons (Prepare Ahead)
Slowly *confit* the duck legs in olive oil over a low heat (approximately 60°C) for 1½ hours, until golden.

Allow the duck leg to cool, then shred and roll into balls of approximately 50g. Dip in flour, then the egg and finally the breadcrumbs. Keep in the fridge.

For The Duck Eggs (Prepare Ahead)
Boil the eggs for 7 minutes in boiling water. Plunge straight into ice water and leave for 10 minutes. Peel, then coat in breadcrumbs, as you did with the bonbons, and reserve in the fridge.

For The Duck *Jus* (Allow Up To 9 Hours)
Pan roast the duck bones to brown them. Add the vegetables to the pan and cook until softened. Cover with water and simmer for 6-8 hours. Strain, return to the pan adding the red wine and reduce until thickened.

For The Duck Breast
Preheat the oven to 180°C (fan).

Score the duck breasts and remove any excess sinew. Place in a cold, dry ovenproof pan and cook until the skin is crisp. Turn, then place in the oven for 10 minutes. Rest the breast for 6-7 minutes.

For The Butternut Squash
Cook the butternut squash with butter until slightly soft. Add the vegetable stock and cook until tender. Blitz to form a smooth purée.

For The Vegetables
Place the potatoes in boiling water and cook until soft. Drain, then colour in a pan with butter. Add the peas into the pan with the potatoes and, when hot, serve.

Pan fry the ceps in olive oil and finish with butter.

To Serve
Deep fry the eggs and leg bonbons at 160°C for 4-5 minutes. Slice the duck breast. Arrange on plates as pictured.

HERB CRUSTED LAMB, POTATO GRATIN PUREE

SERVES 4

*Tomàs Cusiné Vilosell
(Spain)*

Ingredients

Lamb
4 bone rack of lamb
2 rumps of lamb

Potato Gratin Purée
5 large Maris Pipers (peeled)
1 head garlic (chopped)
1 bunch thyme (picked)
1 tsp salt
freshly ground black pepper
125ml double cream

Vegetables
100g peas
100g samphire
100g sweetcorn
1 tbsp olive oil

Herb Crust
1 bunch coriander
4 generous portions rustic bread

large baking tray (greased)

Method

For The Lamb
Preheat the oven to 180°C (fan).

To prep the lamb rack, take any excess meat off the bones, scrape and score the fat, then score the fat of the rump. Pan fry both pieces until golden, cook the rack in the oven for 14 minutes and the rump for 16 minutes. Leave to rest.

For The Potato Gratin Purée
Preheat the oven to 180°C (fan).

Slice the potatoes on a mandolin to approximately 1-3mm. Mix with the salt, pepper, garlic and thyme. Layer in the baking tray and cover with the cream. Bake for 1 hour, then pass through a potato ricer to make a purée.

For The Herb Crust
Preheat the oven to 100°C (fan).

Place the bread in a food processor with the coriander and blitz until very fine. Spread onto a baking tray and cook for 10 minutes to dry out. Set aside.

For The Vegetables
Mix the peas, samphire and sweetcorn in a pan with a tablespoon of olive oil and cook until the samphire is slightly wilted.

To Serve
Swipe the purée over the plate, slice the rack and rump. Dip one side of the rack in the herb crust. Arrange on the plate with a line of the pea, samphire and sweetcorn mix. Drizzle with juices from the lamb.

RASPBERRY GEL, LEMON CURD, PASTILLE, CHOCOLATE SPHERE, BROWNIE

SERVES 6

 Kayena Botrytris Riesling
(Tasmania, Australia)

Ingredients

Raspberry Gel

300g raspberry purée
50g dried agar

Lemon Curd

4 lemons (zest and juice of)
175g caster sugar
110g butter
4 eggs

Pastille

500g fruit raspberry purée
180g glucose
20g pectin
300g caster sugar (plus extra to coat)

Chocolate Sphere

250g 70% chocolate

Brownie (enough for 8-12 portions)

140g 70% chocolate
225g butter
450g caster sugar
5 eggs
110g plain flour
55g cocoa powder

To Serve

100g pistachios (12 left whole to garnish
brownie, remainder to be crushed)

12 half sphere moulds for chocolate spheres
(12 half sphere mould tray - $^{1}/_{3}$ gastronome size,
or you can use small, rounded bowls lined with
cling film)
26x38cm baking tray for brownie (greased)
20x20cm mould for pastille

Method

For The Raspberry Gel

Heat the purée and add the agar. Cook until smooth. Spread thinly and evenly over a silicone mat, leave for 30 minutes in the fridge and cut into strips.

For The Lemon Curd

Melt the butter, sugar and lemon juice over a simmering pan of water (*bain-marie*). Don't let the water touch the bowl. When the sugar has dissolved and the butter has melted, add the eggs and cook until it thickens, stirring continuously.

For The Chocolate Sphere

Melt the chocolate over a *bain-marie*. Pour into the mould until full then pour out until all the chocolate has run out. Scrape the mould with a palette knife and leave to set at room temperature.

For The Brownie

Preheat the oven to 190°C (fan).

Melt the chocolate over a *bain-marie* Add the butter and sugar and when dissolved, add the eggs, flour and cocoa powder. Combine well then place into a baking tray and into the oven for 30-40 minutes. When cooked but still soft, remove from oven, leave to cool and slice into cubes.

For The Pastille

Bring the purée and glucose up to 107°C. Remove from the heat, add the sugar and pectin, stir well, then bring back to 107°C. Pour into a heatproof mould to set at room temperature. When set, cube and roll in sugar. Store in an airtight container in the freezer.

To Serve

Take a strip of gel and place on the plate and top with the pistachios and pastille. Fill the sphere with lemon curd and the brownie, top with 3 pistachios and place the lid on top. Although a lid is not shown in the picture there will be enough chocolate spheres to use for this if desired.

Chef's Tip

All elements of this dish may be prepared ahead and assembled when required.

140 LLANSANTFFRAED COURT HOTEL & RESTAURANT

Clytha, Llanvihangel Gobion, Abergavenny, NP7 9BA

01873 840 678
www.llch.co.uk

Llansantffraed Court is a 4 star country house hotel, set in 20 acres of stunning parkland, in the foodie golden triangle of rural Monmouthshire, and on the edge of the Brecon Beacons National Park and the Wye Valley. The rather grand stately exterior belies the unstuffy and warm nature of the welcome Mike Morgan and his team offer. This is very much a food-led hotel. They have a huge restored Victorian walled vegetable garden which drives the seasonality of the menus and they are champions of local ingredient sourcing, making the most of the area's abundance of passionate artisan food suppliers.

Expect a genuine friendly 'Croeso', easy comfort and a focus on the very best locally sourced food cooked to exacting modern fine dining standards. The many years of Michelin starred experience in the kitchen brigade make the dining offer look deceptively simple, with accurate cooking, stunning presentation and clear flavours the backbone of a now highly regarded dining room at accessible prices.

The beamed dining room, decorated in a muted classic modern style with quality table linen and high end glassware, is the perfect backdrop for the food. Together with comfortable lounges, open fires, a south facing sunny terrace overlooking the lake, and a carefully chosen 200 bin wine list, with every single wine available by the glass, makes it a perfect place for a short break.

Llansantffraed has a hard earned reputation for high standard, locally sourced food, reflected by its impressive list of accolades. It has retained 2 AA Rosettes for 18 consecutive years, been listed in the Michelin Guide for the same period, shortlisted for AA Wine List of the Year for the last eight years and won Best Small Restaurant in the National Tourism Awards for Wales in 2013 - recognition that is commensurate with the passion shown in every plate and glass served at Llansantffraed.

Relish Restaurant Rewards
See page 007 for details.

Present holder of the Winner's Award for Best Small Restaurant in the National Tourism Awards. As it was chosen by an open public vote, this is an accolade of which the team are justifiably proud.

CLYTHA ESTATE WOOD PIGEON, BEETROOT, HAZELNUT, WILD MUSHROOM

SERVES 4

Guy Allion, 'Les Parcs', Pinot Noir, 2011 (France)

Ingredients

Pigeon Breasts

8 pigeon breasts
1 sprig rosemary (finely chopped)
1 sprig thyme (finely chopped)
salt and pepper

Beetroot Purée

5 large beetroots (peeled, evenly chopped)
50g shallots (peeled)
50g sugar
500ml chicken stock
50ml sherry vinegar

Baby Beetroot

16 baby beetroots (cooked)
50g unsalted Welsh butter
50ml chicken stock

Mushrooms

100g Forest Blewitt mushrooms
100g Pied de Mouton mushrooms
unsalted Welsh butter (knob of)

Parsnip Crisps

1 parsnip (peeled)
oil (to deep fry)

Garnish

50g hazelnuts (roasted, crushed)
foraged leaves

Method

For The Beetroot Purée

Cook the chopped beetroots in water until tender, then drain. In a separate pan, sweat the shallots in a little oil. Add the cooked beetroots along with the stock and sugar. Reduce until almost all the stock has evaporated. Add the sherry vinegar. Blitz in a processor.

> **Chef's Tip**
> Place purée in a squeezy bottle to help make neat designs on the plate.

For The Pigeon Breasts

Season the pigeon with salt, pepper and the herbs. Seal in a vacuum pack bag and cook at 62°C for 5 minutes. Remove breasts and allow them to rest. Pan fry in a hot pan for 1 minute each side. Alternative method: Heat a little oil in a pan. Pan fry the breasts for 2 minutes on each side, finish with a knob of butter.

For The Mushrooms

Sauté the mushrooms in a little oil until each side is coloured. Finish with a little butter and seasoning.

For The Parsnip Crisps

Use a peeler to make fine strips of parsnip. Deep fry in hot oil (160°C) until golden brown.

For The Baby Beetroot

Gently heat the baby beetroots, chicken stock and butter.

To Assemble

Dress the plate with some of the beetroot purée. Sprinkle some of the crushed hazelnuts on each plate. Arrange the mushrooms, parsnip crisps and baby beetroots on the plate. Cut the pigeon breasts in half lengthways and place attractively on the plate. Garnish with foraged leaves.

BRECON LAMB LOIN & BREAST, ARTICHOKES, SAMPHIRE

SERVES 4

 Ladybird, Cabernet Sauvignon, Cabernet Franc, Merlot, 2011 (South Africa)

Ingredients

Lamb Loin

1 lamb loin (cut into 4 x 150g portions)
4 sprigs rosemary
2 cloves garlic

Lamb Breast

2 lamb breasts
2 sprigs rosemary
1 clove garlic (chopped)

Artichokes

10 Jerusalem artichokes
300ml milk
4 globe artichokes
3 lemons (juice of)

Artichoke Crisps

1 Jerusalem artichoke

To Serve

100g crosnes
100g samphire grass
50g unsalted Welsh butter
50ml chicken stock

Method

For The Lamb Loin

Prepare and portion the lamb loin, making sure no skin is left on the outside and the fat is neatly trimmed. Put in individual vacuum bags with the rosemary and half a clove of garlic. Seal and cook for 18 minutes at 63°C.

Alternative method: Place the portioned lamb in a hot pan, with the herbs, and allow the fat to render down. Cook over a medium heat for 4-5 minutes, basting regularly. Leave to rest.

For The Artichoke Purée

Peel 6 of the Jerusalem artichokes and chop evenly. Add these to a pan with milk, then cook until soft. Blitz in a processor and season.

For The Artichokes

Globes: Peel off the outer leaves using a small knife, then remove the outer stem with a peeler. Drizzle with lemon juice. Cook in salted water until soft for around 7 minutes.

Jerusalems: Peel the remaining Jerusalem artichokes and cook in salted water with the juice of 1 lemon.

> **Chef's Tip**
> Lemon juice stops the artichokes from turning brown.

For The Lamb Breast (Prepare Ahead)

Trim any excess fat off the breasts. Seal in vacuum bags with 1 clove of chopped garlic and 2 sprigs of rosemary. Cook for 12 hours at 72°C. Alternative method: *Confit* the lamb breast by placing the breast, garlic and rosemary in an ovenproof dish, cover with vegetable oil and cook in the oven at 130°C for 4 hours.

For The Artichoke Crisps

Thinly slice the Jerusalem artichokes. Deep fry in oil at 160°C until crisp and golden.

To Assemble

Place the lamb loin, fat side down, in a hot pan. Gently render the fat until crisp and golden. Turn the lamb until brown on all sides. In a separate pan, gently heat the breast until golden on all sides.

Heat artichokes and crosnes until lightly caramelised on all sides, add chicken stock and butter to glaze, then add the samphire at the last minute as it will cook quickly. Squeeze a little of the purée on the plate, arrange the lamb breast, artichokes and samphire, then top with lamb loin. Finish with *jus* and artichoke crisps.

ASSIETTE OF LEMON & RHUBARB

SERVES 4

Late Harvest Sauvignon Blanc, 2011
(Chile)

Ingredients

Lemon Custard

3 eggs
100g sugar
2 lemons (juice and zest)
120ml double cream

Mascarpone Cream

100g mascarpone
1 vanilla pod (seeds removed)
100g icing sugar

Poached Rhubarb

150g rhubarb (washed, peeled)
100ml stock syrup
25ml grenadine

Rhubarb Sorbet

250g rhubarb (washed, peeled)
250ml stock syrup
50g glucose

4 ramekins or loose bottomed moulds
(lined with cling film)

Method

For The Lemon Custard

Whip together the eggs and sugar, add the lemon and cream. Spoon into lined moulds and cook at 120°C for 12-15 minutes or until set. Chill in the fridge.

For The Mascarpone Cream

Mix mascarpone, vanilla seeds and icing sugar together until smooth.

For The Poached Rhubarb

Cut the rhubarb into batons. Gently poach it in the stock syrup and grenadine until soft.

> **Chef's Tip**
> Cooking rhubarb with some grenadine keeps the rhubarb nice and pink.

For The Rhubarb Sorbet

Blitz or juice the rhubarb, then pass the juice through muslin. Combine equal quantities of juice and stock syrup with 50g glucose and churn in an ice cream machine. Freeze until required.

To Assemble

Swipe some of the mascarpone cream on the plate. Remove lemon custard from the ramekins and place on top of the mascarpone. Arrange some of the rhubarb pieces on top of the lemon custard. Garnish with some rhubarb sorbet.

150
MANORHAUS LLANGOLLEN

Hill Street, Llangollen, Denbighshire, LL20 8EU

01978 860 775
www.manorhaus.com Twitter: @manorhaus

n the heart of the bustling Welsh town of Llangollen, amidst the Victorian steam railway, the dramatic River Dee and the stately elegance of Plas Newydd house and gardens, you'll discover manorhaus Llangollen - a Victorian building recently transformed into a boutique restaurant-with-rooms. The stylish interiors reflect the monochromatic nature of many of the buildings in the town and add a decadent splash of colour; from the vivid orange front door and bar furniture to the daffodil yellow tiles of the bathrooms.

Each of the six bedrooms is complemented by Melin Tregwynt fabrics, Egyptian cotton bedding, fluffy towels and locally handmade toiletries as well as photographs of the town; sense of place is paramount and the view from the four suites of Castell Dinas Bran gives a further nod to the heritage of the area. Relax in the rooftop hot tub where stunning views can be soaked up come rain or shine; this facility is booked for private use.

And with such rich and verdant surroundings, great food is certainly on the menu with the Dee Valley offering an amazing resource for seasonal and regional ingredients that offer classic dishes with a contemporary twist; from Welsh Black beef and Dee Valley lamb, Welsh sea trout and Welsh cheeses.

The small kitchen team relishes making most dishes from scratch; stocks, sauces, ice cream, sorbets, biscuits for cheese and petit-fours all are made in-house and show passion and innovation as well as celebrating the art of good cooking and quality ingredients. The restaurant is an oasis of calm offering an informal, friendly yet attentive service which accompanies a frequently changing set-priced menu.

This is the second project for owners Christopher Frost and Gavin Harris who created the original award-winning manorhaus in Ruthin, and manorhaus Llangollen was awarded an Arts and Business Award in 2013 for innovation in collaboration with local artists to provide newly-commissioned artworks for the property.

There is a plethora of outdoor activities on the doorstep; canoeing on the River Dee, barge trips across the UNESCO World Heritage Pontycysyllte Aqueduct, trekking the Offa's Dyke Path and cycling the Horse Shoe Pass. Plas Newydd, once home to the 'Ladies of Llangollen', is just around the corner and offers a peek into a bygone age. The town is part of the Clywdian Range 'Area of Outstanding Natural Beauty'. The town has a reputation for hosting festivals and events throughout the year, attracting headline acts from across the globe.

Relish Restaurant Rewards
See page 007 for details.

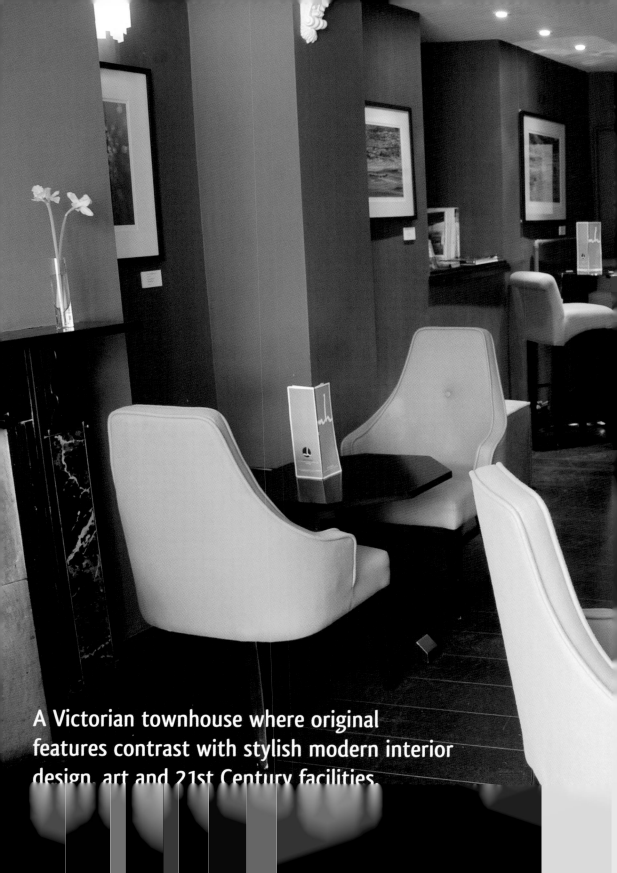

A Victorian townhouse where original
features contrast with stylish modern interior
design, art and 21st Century facilities.

BUTTERNUT SQUASH & PERL WEN CREPE

SERVES 4

 Sipp Mack Pinot Blanc 2010
(Alsace, France)

Ingredients

Butternut Squash Filling

½ butternut squash (peeled, seeded, cubed)
3 sprigs thyme
100g Perl Wen or brie (cut into small pieces)

Crêpes

110g plain flour (sifted)
salt (pinch of)
2 medium eggs
200ml milk
75ml water
25g butter (melted)

Emulsion

200ml carrot juice
salt and pepper
200ml single cream

Garnish

rocket
pine nuts
orange syrup

4 ramekin dishes (lightly buttered)

Method

For The Butternut Squash

Preheat the oven to 180°C.

Place the cubed squash into a shallow tray with the thyme. Roast until golden and tender, about 20-25 minutes.

For The Crêpes

Sift the flour into a bowl with the salt. Combine the water and milk. Beat the eggs and melted butter into the milk mixture. Gradually beat the liquid into the flour to ensure no lumps.

Heat a heavy bottomed frying pan or skillet with some melted butter and pour in enough batter to create a thin, 18cm diameter pancake. Cook until lightly golden and flip to cook the other side. Set to one side and continue to cook a further 3 pancakes.

Carefully place a crêpe into the ramekin, ensuring the base is covered, and pleat the sides. Add some butternut squash in the base of each crêpe, top with cubes of cheese, followed by squash until loosely packed in. Carefully fold over the crêpe sides to ensure the top is covered.

> **Chef's Tip**
> The crêpes and filling can be made, filled and cling filmed in advance. Refrigerate to store.

For The *Emulsion*

Simmer the carrot juice and seasoning in a pan until reduced by half. Add the cream and simmer until thickened to a velvety texture to coat the back of a spoon.

To Serve

Preheat the oven to 180°C.

Place the ramekins into the oven for 12-15 minutes until thoroughly heated through. Run a blade around the crêpe edge to release from the ramekin and carefully turn out into a shallow bowl. Pour some *emulsion* around the side. Top with some rocket and pine nuts then drizzle with a little orange syrup.

TWICE COOKED PORK BELLY WITH BLACK PUDDING FRITTERS, TARTE TATIN & TAFFY CIDER SAUCE

SERVES 4

 *Bladen Marlborough Pinot Noir 2010
(New Zealand)*

Ingredients

For The Pork And Cider Stock

1.8kg pork belly
1 bulb garlic (crushed)
50g butter (softened)
10 sage leaves (chopped)
seasoning
2 sticks celery (quartered)
2 carrots (quartered)
1 white onion (quartered)
330ml bottle Taffy's cider or similar dry cider

Tarte Tatin

2 small Cox apples (cored, sliced)
6 x 5cm diameter cut circles puff pastry
2 knobs butter (melted)

For The Fritters

1 x 200g individual Bury black pudding
50g plain flour
50g cornflour
125ml soda water
oil (for frying)

Taffy Cider Sauce

cider stock (see above)
200ml cream

To Serve

carrot purée
wilted cabbage

Method

For The Pork Belly (Prepare At Least 2 Days Before)

Combine the garlic, butter, sage and seasoning and rub to baste the pork. Place in a roasting dish on top of the vegetables and pour over the cider. Refrigerate overnight allowing the flavours to infuse.

Preheat the oven to 180°C.

Cover the roasting dish with foil, place in the oven for 3 hours.

Remove from oven and allow to cool. Carefully slice off the pork skin, cling wrap the pork belly and refrigerate overnight, or for up to 3 days. Skim off any excess cold fat from the roasting juices and vegetables, then transfer cider stock and vegetables to a container. The stock may also be kept in the fridge for up to 3 days.

For The Apple Tarte Tatin

Preheat the oven to 180°C.

Heat some butter in a shallow pan and *sauté* the apple slices to colour.

Place the puff pastry rounds on a greased baking sheet and carefully top with a fan of apple slices. Brush with the melted butter. Bake in the oven for 15 minutes until the pastry is risen and golden.

For The Fritters

Combine the flour, cornflour and some seasoning with soda water to create a thick batter. Roll the black pudding meat into 2½cm balls and coat with the batter. Deep fry until golden in a fryer, or in a shallow frying pan with oil.

For The Taffy Cider Sauce

Reheat the cider stock and vegetables and simmer for 10 minutes, before straining to remove the vegetables. Continue to simmer to reduce the liquid by half before adding the cream. Season to taste.

To Serve

Preheat the oven to 180°C.

Cut the pork belly into 2½cm thick slices. In a hot ovenproof pan with some butter, sear each side of the slices before placing in the oven for 15 minutes. Serve as pictured with seasonal vegetables.

Chef's Tip

Pork skin can be roasted in a hot oven to make crackling.

GLUTEN FREE LEMON & BLUEBERRY POLENTA CAKE WITH BLUEBERRY ICE CREAM

SERVES 8

 Quady Elysium Black Muscat 2009
(California, USA)

Ingredients

Lemon And Blueberry Cake

200g unsalted butter (soft)
200g caster sugar
200g ground almonds
100g fine polenta
1½ tsp baking powder (gluten free)
3 large eggs
2 lemons (zest, juice of)
200g blueberries
125g icing sugar

Blueberry Ice Cream

330g frozen blueberries
100g caster sugar
150ml single cream

Garnish

sugared lemon zest
shortbread biscuit (gluten free)

23cm springform cake tin (lined with baking
paper, lightly greased)

Method

For The Lemon And Blueberry Cake

Preheat the oven to 180°C.

Cream the butter and caster sugar until pale and whipped. Mix the almonds, polenta and baking powder together and beat some of this into the butter-sugar mixture, followed by 1 egg, then alternate dry ingredients and eggs, beating as you go.

Beat in the lemon zest and fold in three quarters of the blueberries. Pour the mixture into your tin and tap the tin to level the mixture. Place the remaining blueberries evenly around the top of the mixture and bake in the oven for about 40 minutes. Use a cake tester to check middle is cooked.

Make a syrup by boiling together the lemon juice and icing sugar in a small saucepan until the sugar has dissolved.

Prick the top of the cake all over with a cake tester and pour the warm syrup over the cake. Leave to cool before taking it out of the tin.

For The Blueberry Ice Cream

Blend the frozen berries and sugar in a food processor, then with the mixer set to slow, pour in the cream until well combined. Serve immediately or freeze until needed.

To Serve

Assemble as pictured.

> **Chef's Tip**
> Use raspberries or blackberries for delicious alternatives.

160
THE OLD RECTORY

Llangattock, Crickhowell, Powys, NP8 1PH

01873 810 373
www.rectoryhotel.co.uk

Youth and experience has helped create a winning combination for one of Wales' 'must-visit' restaurants.

The Old Rectory, at Llangattock, near Crickhowell, is owned by the Ellis family and showcases the culinary skills of head chef Dave Chamberlain.

Father and daughter team Shaun and Sophie Ellis oversee operations - Shaun is one of the region's most experienced chefs and has worked in most of its fine dining restaurants.

They work with head chef Dave Chamberlain to give guests a taste of the region. Well-travelled, Dave worked in some of Europe's best kitchens before returning to his beloved Wales. Stints with Gordon Ramsay and Marcus Wareing at Claridges, Royal Hospital Road, Petrus and The Savoy Grill equipped him to cook at 2 and 3 Michelin star standard. He also dazzled Michel Roux Jr by securing a last five spot on BBC TV's MasterChef: The Professionals.

The Old Rectory is a country hotel which dates back to the 16th Century and was formerly the home of the celebrated poet Henry Vaughan.

It sits within the exceptionally pretty Brecon Beacons National Park and is surrounded by verdant, rolling countryside.

The Black Mountains provide a sumptuous backdrop and the hotel is popular with diners, wedding parties and golfers, who make full use of The Old Rectory's own course.

The Ellis family took over operations in 2012 and have already overseen substantial improvements, with a refurbishment of its restaurant now complete.

Sophie said: "We're in a stunning location and we're very proud of what we do. We aim to provide our guests with a comfortable, carefree environment in which to relax and enjoy the best of regional food."

The hotel has exceptional contacts with the region's finest food producers who regularly knock on the kitchen door, armed with the finest seasonal ingredients.

 Relish Restaurant Rewards
See page 007 for details.

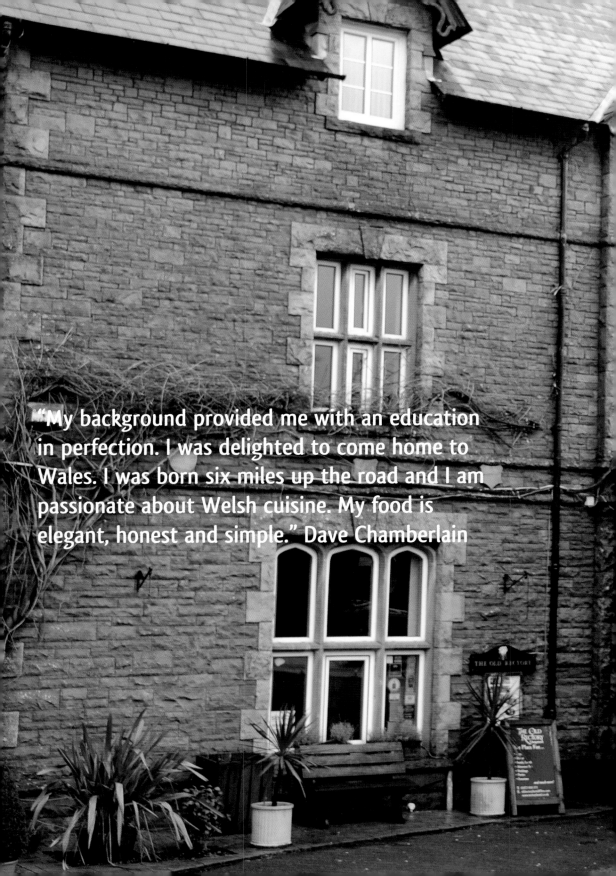

"My background provided me with an education in perfection. I was delighted to come home to Wales. I was born six miles up the road and I am passionate about Welsh cuisine. My food is elegant, honest and simple." Dave Chamberlain

DUO OF TUNA CARPACCIO, TOASTED POPPY SEEDS, MUSTARD, PICKLED VEGETABLES & PICKLED GINGER

SERVES 4

 *2010 Pinot Noir, Fronholz, Alsace
(France)*

Ingredients

1kg tuna loin (sushi grade)
50g poppy seeds
50g wholegrain mustard
50ml olive oil

Pickled Vegetables

½ cucumber
1 beetroot

Pickling Liquor

1 cup white wine vinegar
1 star anise
10 pink peppercorns
1 bay leaf
10 juniper berries
1 cup cold water
1 cup caster sugar
2 tbsp rock salt

Japanese Marinade

50ml sesame oil
50ml dark soy sauce
50ml rice vinegar
60ml fish sauce
50ml light soy sauce
salt (pinch of)
1 lime (juice of)

To Serve

5g pink pickled ginger
cress
pea shoots or leaves

Method

For The Pickled Vegetables (Prepare 2 hours ahead)

Grate the beetroot and cucumber and place in a heatproof dish.

Add all the pickling ingredients into a pan and bring to the boil. Pour over the cucumber and beetroot and place in the fridge to cool.

For The Tuna

Cut the tuna loin in half, lengthways. Cut one half into a 5cm cylinder shape. This will be used for your seared carpaccio.

Cut the other half very thinly and put to one side. This is for you to roll out later.

> **Chef's Tip**
> Always use the freshest of fish and season it well.

For The Japanese Marinade (Prepare Ahead)

Put all ingredients in a bowl and whisk until they come together. Add a pinch of salt and leave to one side.

For The Sliced Tuna

Place the thin slices of tuna between sheets of parchment paper and roll out with a rolling pin until very thin. Cut into rectangular pieces (as seen in the photograph). Marinate in the Japanese marinade whilst you are preparing the carpaccio.

For The Tuna Carpaccio

Heat a non-stick pan with a tiny bit of olive oil. When hot, add the cylinder shaped tuna and sear for 7 seconds on each side, then place on a cooling rack. Return the pan to the heat and add the poppy seeds and toast lightly. Place the toasted seeds in a tray alongside a tray of mustard. Roll the cooled tuna in the mustard and then again in the toasted poppy seeds. Once this is done, wrap in cling film.

To Assemble

Place a rectangular piece of tuna on each plate and add a dressing of pink ginger. Layer the pickled vegetables. Slice the seared tuna steak into 2½cm slices and place 3 slices on each plate. Dress with cress or leaves.

POACHED MONKFISH WITH WILD MUSHROOM RISOTTO & ASPARAGUS

SERVES 4

2011 Pinot Gris, Rotenberg
(France)

Ingredients

Poached Monkfish

4 x 400g monkfish portions
4 slices Parma ham
8 leaves basil
salt and pepper

Risotto

2 shallots (diced)
2 cloves garlic (crushed)
50ml olive oil
400g wild mixed mushrooms
400g Arborio rice
1 litre chicken stock
500ml white wine
salt and pepper
6 spears asparagus (tips removed for garnish,
remainder sliced)
500g spinach
50g butter
150g Parmesan cheese

Sherry Vinegar Caramel

10ml water
60g sugar
50ml sherry vinegar

To Serve

mushrooms (deep fried at 180°C)
sherry vinegar caramel (drizzle of)
asparagus spear tips (steamed)

Method

To Poach The Monkfish

Trim all sinews off the monkfish.

Place 2 basil leaves on each monkfish fillet, season, then wrap each fillet individually in Parma ham. Wrap each portion of fillet well in cling film. Poach in boiling water for 6½ minutes, then place in a bowl of ice cold water to chill.

For The Wild Mushroom Risotto

Heat a heavy bottomed pan, add a little olive oil, shallots and garlic, and *sauté* uncovered. Once soft, add the wild mushrooms and the remainder of the oil. Gently *sauté* the mushrooms until they are cooked, then add the rice. Stir for 1 minute. Gradually add the stock and wine, ladle by ladle and continue cooking, stirring, until the rice has absorbed nearly all the liquid. Add the sliced asparagus and spinach, season to taste and serve when ready. Don't forget to add the Parmesan and butter at the last minute.

For The Sherry Vinegar Caramel (Can Be Prepared Ahead)

Place the sugar and water into a small pan and, over a low heat, allow the sugar to melt without stirring it. Once fully dissolved, add the sherry vinegar, stir, bring to the boil then remove from the heat. Allow to cool. Store in a squeezy bottle, in the fridge, until needed.

To Finish The Monkfish

Preheat the oven to 170°C. (non fan)

Remove the cling film from the monkfish. Sear the fillets in a hot pan, then place in the oven for approximately 6 minutes. Slice and serve.

To Assemble

Pick 4 of your best plates. Drizzle the plate with the sherry vinegar caramel. Arrange the risotto on the plate and place the sliced monkfish on top. Garnish with steamed fresh asparagus tips and deep fried mushrooms.

> **Chef's Tip**
> Try to use a homemade chicken stock as it will give a better flavour.

ASSIETTE OF CHOCOLATE

SERVES 8

 Cloudy Bay Late Harvest Riesling 2007
(New Zealand)

Ingredients

Brownie (serves 8-12)

200g dark chocolate 70%
200g butter
6 whole eggs
70g 100% cocoa powder
285ml Baileys
450g caster sugar
200g plain flour
50g white chocolate callets or buttons
icing sugar (to dust, optional)

Tia Maria Jelly

4 shots Tia Maria
400ml cranberry juice
2 tbsp granulated coffee
100g caster sugar
2 leaves gelatine (soaked)

White Chocolate And Orange Mousse

200g white chocolate
4 egg whites
100g icing sugar
200ml double cream
1 large orange (zest of)

Dark Chocolate Brûlée

250ml double cream
1 vanilla pod (split and scraped)
200g dark chocolate 70%
1 shot brandy
5 egg yolks
100g caster sugar
caster sugar (for topping)

Garnish

fresh raspberries
melted chocolate (to decorate plate)
raspberry coulis (to decorate plate)

26 x 38cm deep sided baking tray (greased)
8 espresso cups
8 shot glasses

Method

For The Brownie

Preheat the oven to 160°C.

Melt the chocolate and butter together in a *bain-marie*. Place the eggs and sugar in a bowl and beat until light and fluffy. When the chocolate has melted, combine all ingredients together (other than white chocolate buttons) and mix well. When the mixture has cooled, stir in the white chocolate. Pour into the baking tray and bake for 40 minutes or until the brownie starts cracking on the top.

For The Tia Maria Jelly

Place the first 4 ingredients into a pan and bring to a simmer. Add the softened gelatine and stir until it has melted. Allow the mixture to cool and pour into shot glasses to 2½cm deep. Leave to set in the fridge for 2 hours.

For The White Chocolate And Orange Mousse

Melt the white chocolate in a *bain-marie*. Whisk the egg whites with the sugar until stiff like a meringue. In a separate bowl, whisk the double cream with the orange zest to a soft peak. Fold the chocolate into the cream, then at the final stage, fold in the egg whites. Put into a piping bag and pipe on top of the Tia Maria jelly. Garnish with fresh raspberries.

For The Dark Chocolate Brûlée

Add the cream and vanilla into a pan then heat gently. Melt the chocolate with the brandy in a *bain-marie*. In a separate bowl, whisk the egg yolks and sugar together until light and fluffy. Once the vanilla cream has come to the boil, add it to the eggs and sugar, whisking rapidly. Add the melted chocolate, whisk well. Return to a clean pan and place back on the heat until the mixture starts forming a custard-like consistency. Pass through a sieve, then pour into your espresso cups. Set in the fridge for up to 3 hours. Just before serving, dust with sugar and grill or use a blow torch to brûlée.

To Serve

Assemble as in the picture.

> **Chef's Tip**
> All elements of this dessert can be made the day before and kept in the fridge. However, keep the brownie at room temperature as it will taste better.

170
PARK HOUSE

20 Park Place, Cardiff CF10 3DQ

02920 224 343
www.parkhouserestaurant.co.uk

ine dining and sumptuous wines in one of Britain's most spectacular dining rooms helps Park House stand out from the crowd.

A starry culinary offering with Wales' finest wine list and a Grade I listed dining room make the Cardiff venue one of a kind.

Its exceptional, pan-British menu is overseen by head chef Jonathan Edwards and Michelin starred consultant chef Roger Jones, from The Harrow, at Little Bedwyn.

Jones, who has held a star for eight years, was formerly the youngest ever head chef for The Queen, and he works alongside talented head chef Jonathan Edwards, developing the Park House team.

The venue is aiming for the stars, with owners Adam and Claire Pledger building an impressive reputation.

Park House is housed in the 150-year-old Grade I listed William Burges-designed building, which is a romantic gothic masterpiece. Original oak panels and intricate cornicing are redolent of a golden era.

Adam says: "We provide an unrivalled food offering, but we also have the best wine list in Wales - and one of the best wine lists in the UK. We're very passionate about great food being matched with great wines. Park House is an oenophile."

Park House won the AA Wine List of the Year - Wales for 2013/14 and also won the Wine Spectator Award of Excellence.

It provides diners with a unique experience across three floors: Canapés are served in the wine bar, Pinot, while the venue also has one of the funkiest cocktail bars in the UK called Vanilla Rooms.

"We provide a unique dining experience," adds Adam. "The best food, the greatest wines and the most unique restaurant. We are a true one-off."

Relish Restaurant Rewards
See page 007 for details.

What sets Park House apart from most restaurants in Wales and the UK is our passion for food and wine matching. Every dish across all our menus has a carefully selected wine match that enhances the culinary experience.

COCONUT PANNA COTTA & MOJITO SORBET

SERVES 6

 Botrytis Riesling, Heggies Vineyard, Eden Valley
(Australia)

Ingredients

Coconut Panna Cotta

100g white chocolate
600g coconut purée or coconut cream
2-3 sheets leaf gelatine (soaked in cold water
for 5 minutes)

Mango Purée

1 medium mango (peeled, stone removed)
1 tbsp liquid glucose
icing sugar (to taste)

Pineapple Crisps

12 pieces of pineapple (finely sliced)
chilli flakes (to dust)

Pineapple Salsa

1 medium mango (peeled, diced into
1½cm cubes)
1 pineapple (peeled, diced into
1½cm cubes)
1 lime (squeeze of)
1 medium chilli (finely sliced)
3 sprigs mint (finely sliced)
icing sugar (to taste)

Mojito Sorbet

200ml water
200ml sugar
6 medium limes
1 tbsp liquid glucose
1 bunch fresh mint (finely sliced)
1 tbsp white rum

Garnish

10g desiccated coconut (gently toasted)
4 glasses

Method

To Make The Panna Cotta (Make The Day Before)

Gently melt the white chocolate in a heatproof bowl over hot water (*bain-marie*).

Warm the coconut purée in a pan until simmering and remove from the heat.

Squeeze the gelatine to remove any excess water and add to the purée, whisking until melted.

Pour over the melted chocolate and whisk until smooth. Pass through a fine sieve into a jug and allow to cool.

Once cool, pour into glasses and set overnight.

For The Mango Purée

Place the mango in a blender with the glucose and blitz until smooth. Sweeten further with icing sugar if needed. Pass through a fine sieve into a container and chill.

For The Pineapple Crisps (Prepare Ahead)

Preheat the oven to 90°C.

Lay the pineapple slices on a silicone mat lightly dusted with the chilli. Put in the oven for 2-2½ hours until firm and can be easily picked up. Allow to cool and transfer to a container lined with parchment.

For The Pineapple Salsa

Place the mango and pineapple into a bowl with a squeeze of lime. Add the chilli and mint, combine thoroughly. Add icing sugar to taste if needed.

For The Mojito Sorbet

Make a stock syrup by placing the sugar and water into a pan. Slowly bring to the boil, then remove from the heat. Squeeze the limes and put the juice to one side. Put the lime skins and glucose into the stock syrup and allow to infuse for 10-15 minutes. Once cool, pass the lime flavoured syrup through a fine mesh sieve. Add the lime juice and mint along with the rum.

Place in an ice cream machine to churn until frozen. Store in the freezer.

To Serve

Assemble as pictured.

180 PETERSTONE COURT

COUNTRY HOUSE, RESTAURANT, ROOMS & SPA

Llanhamlach, Brecon, Powys, LD3 7YB

01874 665 387
www.peterstone-court.com

An elegant, privately owned Georgian manor house, Peterstone Court enjoys an amazing location overlooking the River Usk, with stunning views across the valley to South Wales' highest peak, Pen-y-Fan.

It should come as no surprise that food lies at the heart of Peterstone Court as it is run and owned by a group of restaurateurs rather than hoteliers. The food is fresh, local and seasonal. Some part of the family are longstanding local farmers and, being located only seven miles away, provide a unique and sustainable arrangement in rearing meat and poultry used in the house kitchens. Everything on the menu is handmade, sourced in season, at its freshest and from the local area.

The restaurant at Peterstone has won many awards for its food including 2 AA Rosettes and is recommended by all the major food guides. Our head chef, Josh Blakemore, prefers to 'keep it simple, focus on taste and flavours', and has a talent for creating dishes which combine traditional favourites with a modern British bistro-style.

Pop in for a coffee, sandwich or a bowl of soup and you are just as likely to be amongst folk who are having a five course leisurely lunch or dinner on the terrace. This is no clichéd country house, the atmosphere is relaxed and informal; oak floors, marble fireplaces, antique furniture and leather armchairs set off with fresh flowers and modern art.

The bedrooms are spacious and relaxing, designed with comfort and luxury in mind. There are eight rooms in the main house and four in the outside, converted stable block, all with crisp bed linen, comfy mattresses, flat screen TV and DVD players.

The fabulous spa and leisure suite, based in the vaulted caverns which were once used as the house cellars, contains a candle-lit meditation room, four-seater sauna, jacuzzi and gym, with a whole range of natural and organic spa treatments on offer.

Outside, there's a heated pool (seasonal), and wooden decks with glorious views of the Brecon Beacons, and you're only a few yards from the world famous hiking and biking trails.

Relish Restaurant Rewards
See page 007 for details.

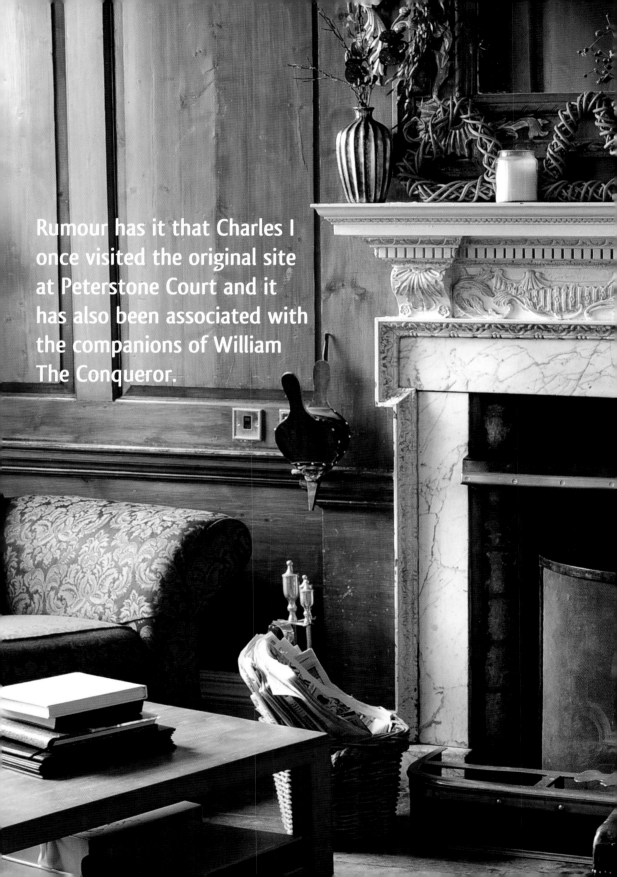

Rumour has it that Charles I once visited the original site at Peterstone Court and it has also been associated with the companions of William The Conqueror.

TWICE BAKED PERL LAS & BROCCOLI SOUFFLE, CONFIT LEEKS, BROCCOLI PUREE, SWEET PICKLED CARROTS

SERVES 6

Primitivo Rosso IGT Salento La Casada
(Italy)

Ingredients

Soufflé

150ml double cream
300ml milk
1 onion (roughly chopped)
3 cloves garlic (roughly chopped)
5 peppercorns
1 bay leaf
1 head broccoli (cut into florets)
bicarbonate of soda (pinch of)
50g butter
50g plain flour
225g Perl Las cheese
6 eggs (separated)

Confit Leeks

100ml white wine
100ml water
100ml sugar
2 leeks (washed, sliced on an angle 1cm thick)

Broccoli Purée

1 head broccoli (cut into small florets)
1 tsp bicarbonate of soda

Pickled Carrots

100ml white wine vinegar
100ml water
100g sugar
3 carrots (turned or batons, cooked for 6 minutes, then plunged into iced water)

6 *dariole* moulds (buttered)

Method

For The Soufflé

Preheat the oven to 150°C (fan).

Heat the cream, milk, onion, garlic, peppercorns and bay leaf in a heavy bottomed pan. Bring to just before boiling point, remove from the heat. Infuse for 15 minutes.

Cook the broccoli with the bicarb until tender, drain and add to a food processor. Strain the milk mixture into the broccoli and blend.

Cook out the butter and flour for 10 minutes. Gradually add the green milk mixture, stirring until it resembles a dropping consistency. You may not need all the milk mixture.

On a low heat, melt in the cheese until smooth. Remove from heat and mix the yolks in well. Cool slightly.

Whisk the egg whites to a soft peak. Fold into the cheese mixture. Place into the moulds up to 1cm from the top. Put into a deep baking tray of cold water. Cook at 150°C for 25-30 minutes. Remove from oven. Once cool, turn out the soufflés.

For The *Confit* Leeks

Bring the wine, water and sugar to a simmer until the sugar dissolves. Add leeks, and leave on a very low heat for 25 minutes. Set pan aside to cool.

For The Broccoli Purée

Put the florets and bicarb in a pan, cover with cold water, cook until soft. Strain, reserving the liquid. Blend the broccoli, season to taste. If it is too thick, add a little of the reserved liquid.

> **Chef's Tip**
> Bicarbonate of soda will stop the broccoli losing its colour during boiling.

For The Pickled Carrots (Make At Least 2 Hours Before)

Add the white wine vinegar, water and sugar to a saucepan and slowly bring to the boil. Meanwhile, in a separate pan of boiling water, add the carrots and boil for 6 minutes. Remove from the boiling water and add them into ice cold water until chilled. Once the pickling liquid has boiled, take it off the heat and add the chilled carrots. Leave to one side for 2 hours to pickle and cool down.

To Serve

Preheat the oven to 180°C. Place soufflés upside down on a baking tray. Bake for 12 minutes until well risen. Serve as pictured.

TRIO OF BRECON PORK CARMARTHEN HAM WRAPPED PORK TENDERLOIN, CONFIT BELLY, FULL WELSH EGG, SHALLOT PUREE, SAGE JUS

SERVES 4

 Cal Y Canto Blanco Vivra
(Spain)

Ingredients

Tenderloin

2 pork tenderloins (trimmed, cut into 2)
8 slices Carmarthen ham
50g wholegrain mustard

Confit Belly

¼ side pork belly
2 carrots (roughly chopped)
1 onion (roughly chopped)
½ bulb garlic (roughly chopped)
2 sticks celery (roughly chopped)
small bunch thyme
1 litre vegetable oil

Full Welsh Egg

4 quail eggs
100g black pudding
50g butter
150g sausage meat
25g flour, 2 eggs (beaten), 100g breadcrumbs
(to coat)

Shallot Purée

25g butter
150g shallots (finely sliced)
50ml cream

Sage *Jus*

1 litre real beef stock, 5 sage leaves
(reduce the stock with the sage until thick,
pass through a sieve)

Chef's Tip
Freezing the quail eggs makes them less fragile and
easier to handle.

Method

For The Pork Tenderloin

Roll out cling film and lay 2 pieces of ham on it, brush with a little mustard, then roll the pork tightly in the ham using the cling film to keep it tight. Tie at each end. Repeat for other pieces of pork.

Poach in a water bath at 63°C for 35 minutes. Cool rapidly under cold running water, set aside. Alternatively, seal on all sides in a hot frying pan, then transfer to the oven (180°C fan) for 15 minutes. Remove from oven, rest for 5 minutes before serving.

For The Belly (Make The Day Before)

Preheat oven to 110°C (fan).

Place all the ingredients in a deep tray, cover with foil and cook for 8 hours. Remove the pork belly and press between 2 trays in the fridge overnight. Portion into 4 pieces.

For The Full Welsh Egg

Cook the eggs in boiling water for 3 minutes then run under cold water until chilled. Gently blend the butter and black pudding in a food processor until pliable.

Place the peeled eggs in the freezer until hard. Gently mould a thin layer of black pudding around the egg, freeze. Add a layer of sausage meat, coat in flour, egg and then breadcrumbs. Store in the fridge.

For The Shallot Purée

Preheat the oven to 150°C (fan).

Cook the shallots in butter until slightly soft, add cream then bring to the boil. Cover and bake for 25 minutes. Blend until smooth. Season to taste.

To Assemble

Preheat the oven to 180°C (fan).

Return the tenderloins to a water bath at 63°C for 15 minutes, remove from cling film and dry with a cloth. Pan fry until golden brown, then transfer to the oven for 5 minutes.

Pan fry the pork belly, skin side down, until golden then transfer to the oven for 10 minutes or until hot.

Deep fry the full Welsh egg until golden brown. Gently slice in half. In separate pans, warm the shallot purée and bring the *jus* to the boil.

JELLY & CREAM
VANILLA BUTTERMILK PUDDING, APPLE JELLY, CONFIT RHUBARB, APPLE & RHUBARB COMPOTE, CRUMBLE TOPPING

SERVES 4

 *Late Harvest Botrytis Riesling, Tamar Ridge
(Tasmania, Australia)*

Ingredients

Buttermilk Pudding

200ml milk
200ml double cream
½ vanilla pod (split lengthways)
6 gelatine leaves (soaked until soft)
100g sugar
300ml buttermilk

Apple Jelly

4 apples (roughly chopped)
500ml good quality apple juice
handful of spinach (washed)
4 gelatine leaves (soaked until soft)

Confit Rhubarb

400g rhubarb (cut into batons)
100g caster sugar
200ml water
3 gelatine leaves (soaked until soft)

Apple And Rhubarb Compôte

3 apples (peeled, diced)
200g rhubarb (diced)
75g caster sugar

Crumble Topping

35g rolled oats
35g plain flour
20g caster sugar
35g butter

4 clear glasses

Method

For The Buttermilk Pudding (Best Made The Day Before)

Heat the milk, cream and vanilla in a large pan until it reaches boiling point, then remove from heat. Leave to infuse. Once cooled slightly, remove the vanilla pod and stir in the sugar, followed by the gelatine. When at room temperature, stir in the buttermilk. Fill a deep tray with uncooked rice and place the glasses in at an angle, gently pour the buttermilk mixture into the glasses until it's just shy of the rim of each glass. Leave to set in the fridge for at least 2 hours.

For The Apple Jelly (Best Made The Day Before)

Cover the apples with apple juice and slowly bring to the boil. Remove the mixture from the heat, leave to infuse for 15 minutes. Strain the juice into a blender with the spinach and blend. Discard the apples. Strain back into a pan over a low heat, add the gelatine and stir until dissolved.

Once the jelly is at room temperature, rotate the glasses at the opposite angle to the buttermilk making sure it is set and gently pour in the apple jelly.

> **Chef's Tip**
> Using spinach will not add any flavour to the apple jelly, but will intensify the colour.

For The *Confit* Rhubarb

Dissolve the sugar in the water and bring to a rapid boil. Add the rhubarb and leave to simmer for 5 minutes. Remove from the heat, leave the rhubarb to soak. Stir in the gelatine.

Once the apple jelly has set, stand the glasses upright and spoon the rhubarb chunks into the centre of the glasses. Pour on a little of the syrup and leave to set in the fridge.

For The Apple And Rhubarb Compôte

Place all ingredients in a pan and cook until the sugar has dissolved and the fruit is soft. Chill the compôte and add on top of the *confit* rhubarb in the glasses.

For The Crumble Topping

Rub the butter and flour together until they form breadcrumbs, add the sugar and oats and bake at 180°C until golden brown, stirring the mixture every 5 minutes.

Cool the crumble topping, then sprinkle over the compôte just before serving.

190
PURPLE POPPADOM

185a Cowbridge Road East, Cardiff, CF11 9AJ

02920 220 026
www.purplepoppadom.com Twitter: @purple_poppadom

Ever since arriving in Wales from London in 2007, Anand George has blazed a culinary trail, his unique brand of Nouvelle Indian Cuisine, winning the young chef countless awards and a growing UK-wide following.

In his early days, Kerala-born chef George described the continent-spanning development of his craft from India to the UK, as a 5,000 mile culinary journey.

Acquiring influences along the way, he formulated a distinct style, a fusion spanning cuisine of the East and West, always challenging the norm, constantly seeking to excite and intrigue his guests. The apotheosis of this journey and crucible for his inspired avant-garde creations, is Purple Poppadom.

His renown began in 2008 when Anand George won the prestigious House of Commons Tiffin Cup for his signature dish Tiffin Sea bass; a deft tower of delicately pan fried fillet nestling on a mustard infused mashed potato in a glossy, tongue tickling sauce of raw mango and ginger.

A stream of innovative dishes has followed the opening of Purple Poppadom in 2011, winning many best restaurant awards in Wales and listings in The Michelin and Good Food guides.

Keen to spread his art at Food Festivals throughout Wales, Anand's fame is growing, attracting praise from leading food critics including Jay Rayner and Tom Parker Bowles.

With an expanding empire, Anand has opened Münchesters, A Gourmet Coffee House in Cardiff and a quirky upmarket Indian takeaway - The Pickled Pepper in Penarth.

But the seedbed of Anand's culinary journey remains Purple Poppadom, his colourful jewel of a restaurant in Canton, where his tight-knit team strives to expand the boundaries of innovative Indian cuisine.

Relish Restaurant Rewards
See page 007 for details.

Multi-award winning chef Anand George in Purple Poppadom, his home of nouvelle Indian cuisine.

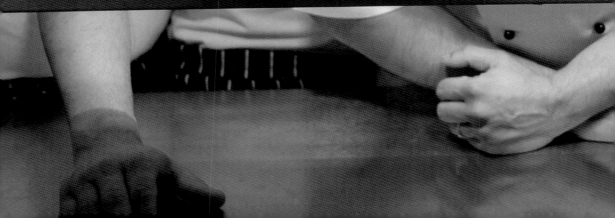

PIDI & THARAVU
DUCK WITH SPICES, PIDI STEAMED RICE DUMPLINGS & SPICED COCONUT SAUCE

SERVES 4

 Allan Scott The Hounds Pinot Noir - Marlborough (New Zealand)

Ingredients

Pidi (Rice Dumpling)

70g rice flour
90ml boiling water
2g salt

Coconut Sauce

40g desiccated coconut
100g Maggi's coconut milk powder
5g salt
300ml water
1g green chilli (chopped)
2g ginger (chopped)
1g cardamom powder, 2g sugar
20ml coconut oil, 2g mustard seeds
2g curry leaves (chopped)
5g shallot (sliced)

Tharavu (Duck)

1kg whole duck (deboned, skinned, cut into small cubes, reserve bones and skin)
100g tomatoes (chopped)
2½cm piece cinnamon
2 green cardamoms, 1g cloves, 2 bay leaves
450g onions (sliced), 8g salt
5g curry leaves (chopped)
10g ginger (chopped)
5g green chilli (chopped)
15g garlic ginger paste (40:60 ratio)
10g coriander powder, 2g turmeric powder
2g garam masala powder
2g ground black pepper
25g Maggi's coconut milk powder (blended with 100ml hot water)
2g fennel powder

Garnish

micro cress

Method

Duck in the classical Syrian Christian style from Kottayam in Kerala.

For The Pidi

Gently dry roast the rice flour over a low heat for approximately 2 minutes, then mix in the salt. Gradually pour the hot water into the rice flour, mix well. Knead to form a soft dough, set aside covered with a wet cloth for 10 minutes.

Divide the dough into 16 small balls, cover again with the wet cloth for 10 minutes. Use them within 30 minutes to stop them drying out. Carefully place the dumplings in 300ml of boiling water, reduce the heat and cook for 5-10 minutes. Strain and add to the coconut sauce.

For The Coconut Sauce

Blitz the desiccated coconut in a grinder to make a fine paste. Mix the coconut paste with the coconut milk powder, salt and water in a pan and bring to the boil, stirring constantly. Add the green chilli, ginger, cardamom powder and sugar. Simmer for approximately 10 minutes.

In a separate pan, heat the coconut oil, add the mustard seeds and allow them to crackle. Add the curry leaves and shallots and *sauté* until it turns light brown. Pour this over the coconut sauce. Gently add in the cooked dumplings and check the seasoning.

For The Duck

Boil the duck bones in water for approximately 1 hour, then add the chopped tomatoes, cinnamon, cardamom, cloves and bay leaves, then simmer for a further 30 minutes. Strain, bring back to the boil then add the cubed duck and cook until it is just done, 10-15 minutes then remove.

Place the duck skin in a pan and allow the fat to melt. Discard the skin and *sauté* the onions, with salt, curry leaves, ginger, green chilli and ginger garlic paste in the fat. Heat on a low temperature until cooked.

Combine the coriander powder, turmeric and black pepper. Pour into the stock and reduce to a sauce consistency. Add in the coconut milk and cooked duck then finish with fennel powder and garam masala powder. Cook for a further 5 minutes.

To Serve

Place the duck in the centre of a plate and arrange 4 of the rice dumplings around the duck, then pour on the coconut sauce. To finish, garnish with micro cress.

TIFFIN SEA BASS, CURRY LEAF MASHED POTATO, ALLEPPEY SAUCE

SERVES 4

 Santiago Ruiz Albariño – Rias Baixas
(Spain)

Ingredients

Alleppey Sauce

300g Maggi coconut milk powder
50ml coconut or vegetable oil
150g onions (sliced)
10g ginger (*julienne*)
150g raw mango (skin and seed removed, cut
into 1cm cubes)
5g curry leaves
20g Kashmiri chilli powder
5g turmeric powder
12g salt
300ml water

Curry Leaf Mash Potato

30ml coconut or vegetable oil
10g split urad dal
5g mustard seeds
10g ginger (chopped)
100g onions (chopped)
5g green chilli (chopped)
5g curry leaves (chopped)
6g salt
2g turmeric powder
450g boiled potatoes (skin removed and grated)
50ml water

Sea Bass

4 sea bass fillets
2g salt
10ml coconut or vegetable oil

Garnish

beetroot pachadi
fried curry leaf

Method

Sea bass fillets, pan seared and served on a bed of curry leaf infused mashed potato; in a tongue tickling Alleppey sauce of raw mango, ginger and coconut.

Anand George's signature dish, commemorating chef's winning of the House of Commons Tiffin Cup in 2008.

For The Alleppey Sauce

Mix the coconut milk powder with 600ml of hot water and blend it well.

Heat the oil in a pan, add sliced onions, ginger, mango and curry leaves, *sauté* until it becomes transparent.

Lower the flame then add the Kashmiri chilli powder, turmeric and salt. *Sauté* for a couple of minutes then add 300ml of water and bring to the boil. When the mixture starts to thicken, add the coconut milk and cook until the sauce consistency is smooth. Take off the heat and pass through a fine sieve and check the seasoning of the sauce.

For The Curry Leaf Mash Potato

Heat the oil in a pan. Add split urad dal and allow it to turn into a golden brown colour. Add mustard seeds, allow to crackle to release flavour, then add the ginger, onion, green chilli and curry leaves. Lower the heat, add turmeric and salt then *sauté* for a minute. Add the water, the boiled potatoes and mash it well. Check seasoning.

For The Sea Bass

Cut the bass fillets into 2, then coat the fillets with salt and oil. Place the bass fillets, skin side down, in a hot pan and cook both sides for approximately 2-3 minutes.

To Serve

Place the sauce on the plate, add the curry leaf mash potato on top. Finally rest the cooked bass fillets on top. Garnish with beetroot pachadi and a fried curry leaf.

ROSE BAPA DOHI, CHOCOLATE SAMOSA, TANDOORI PINEAPPLE

SERVES 4

 Château du Seuil - Cérons, Bordeaux (France)

Ingredients

Rose Bapa Dohi

100g condensed milk
100ml single cream
100ml Greek yoghurt
4g dried rose petals

Chocolate Samosa (Makes 8 pieces)

10g flaked almonds (roasted for 5 minutes at 220°C)
75g Callebaut dark chocolate callets 53.8%
30g unsalted butter
12g caster sugar
30 sheets ready-made spring roll pastry
(25cm square, cut into 16 x 5½cm rectangles)
1 medium egg
oil (for frying)
plain flour (handful of)

Tandoori Pineapple

240g fresh pineapple (cut into 6 pieces of 40g each)
15g vegetable ghee
10g gram flour
5ml saffron water
45g honey
1g green cardamom powder
nutmeg (small pinch of)
170ml single cream

Garnish

fresh raspberries
fresh rose petals
caramelised banana
mixed berry coulis

4 ramekin dishes or ovenproof moulds
4 skewers

Method

For The Rose Bapa Dohi (Prepare 9 Hours In Advance)

Combine all the ingredients together in a bowl and leave to infuse for 4 hours in the fridge.

Strain the mixture and pour into the ramekin dishes. Cover with cling film then place the ramekins in a steamer at 90°C for 20 minutes. Alternatively, carefully place the uncovered dishes in a deep tray filled with water to two thirds of the depth of the ramekins. Place the uncovered tray in the oven at 100°C for 20 minutes.

Once cooled, place the ramekins in the fridge for at least 4 hours to set. Garnish with raspberries and rose petals.

For The Chocolate Samosas (Prepare 12 Hours In Advance)

Preheat the oven to 220°C.

Melt the chocolate, butter, sugar and egg in a *bain-marie*, mixing gently occasionally until it forms a smooth ganache, about 7 minutes. Leave to cool, then add the almond flakes. Mix well, refrigerate for 12 hours.

Divide ganache into 8 equal parts.

Mix some plain flour with water to make a paste to stick the edges of the samosa together which will stop the ganache from oozing out when gently frying.

On the long side of each rectangle of pastry, mark 13cm from the bottom left hand corner. Make a cut from this mark to the top right hand corner. Take 2 rectangles and put them together at right angles to form an L shape with the joining corner 'cut away'. Fold over each leg of the L once to make a pouch. Put in a scoop of the chocolate ganache. Continue folding into a samosa shape, enclosing the ganache mixture. Stick sides well with the flour paste.

Deep fry at 180°C for 30 seconds.

For The Tandoori Pineapple

Heat the vegetable ghee in a heavy bottomed pan and allow it to melt. Lower the heat and slowly add the gram flour, mixing well. Cook through on a low heat for 10 minutes, remove from the heat and allow to cool to a paste.

Combine all the remaining ingredients, except the pineapple, with the paste in a blender. Mix well and pass through a sieve. Marinate the pineapples in the mixture for 3 hours.

Finally, place the pineapple on the skewers and cook in the tandoor oven. Alternatively, preheat the oven to 180°C. Bake the pineapple skewers for 5 minutes. Serve hot.

To Serve

Assemble as pictured.

RESTAURANT 1861

Cross Ash, Abergavenny, NP7 8PB

0845 388 1861 or 01873 821 297
www.18-61.co.uk

Simple, unfussy flavours are to the fore at Restaurant 1861, where chef-proprietor Simon King makes the most of seasonal ingredients.

The acclaimed chef's background as a chef under Michel Roux Senior at the 3 Michelin starred Waterside Inn, is evident in his elegantly presented food.

Simon has a magnificent larder on his doorstep and is able to make the best of seasonal produce from Monmouthshire, as well as the freshest ingredients from his own garden.

"We are fortunate to be located in an area of exceptional produce," says Simon, "we bring classic combinations to the table that showcase immaculate local ingredients."

Simon spent three years at the Waterside Inn before spending a further seven years at the 2 Michelin starred Restaurant Lettonie, with Martin Blunos.

He took a head chef's position at Llansantffraed Court Hotel before becoming chef-proprietor at 1861. His wife, Kate, dedicates herself to the front of house and an ever expanding wine list, while Simon is firmly in control of the kitchen.

Restaurant 1861 is a family business and Simon and Kate's two children live with them on the premises. Kate's father supplies most of the kitchen's fruit and vegetables.

Simon enjoys twice daily deliveries, with salads, herbs and vegetables stunningly fresh. His dishes change with the seasons and guests enjoy his flavoursome food in a light and spacious dining room.

Simon's experience is reflected in every dish, with sophisticated combinations making the best of ingredients.

"We enjoy food that is elegant and reflects the flavours of Monmouthshire."

Relish Restaurant Rewards
See page 007 for details.

MOSAIC OF CITRUS FRUITS, ICED CHOCOLATE PARFAIT

SERVES 4

 Paul Cluver Late Harvest Riesling (South Africa)

Ingredients

Citrus Fruits

1 pink grapefruit
2 blood oranges
1 large orange
3 satsumas
sugar (to taste)
4 leaves bronze gelatine (or an alternative gelling agent)
50ml syrup
50ml grenadine
50ml crème de menthe

Iced Chocolate Parfait

300g sugar
100ml water
250g pasteurised egg yolks
500g dark chocolate (melted)
1 litre double cream (semi-whipped)

Garnish

pomegranate seeds
passion fruit seeds
mint leaves (shredded)

500g terrine mould (lined with cling film)

Method

For The Citrus Fruits (Make The Day Before)

Using a zester, remove the zest from the oranges and reserve.

Segment the grapefruit, oranges, blood oranges and satsumas into a colander over a bowl to catch the juices.

Soak the gelatine in cold water until soft.

Heat the fruit juice gently and dissolve gelatine into the juice, taste and add sugar as required. Strain through a sieve and leave to cool.

Pour a little of the jelly into the base of your terrine mould, then start to layer the fruit randomly into the terrine in layers. Continue with alternating layers of fruit and jelly until all is used.

Cover with cling film and place in the fridge overnight to set.

Blanch the zest in boiling water until tender. Divide into 3 small pots, cover one with grenadine, one with crème de menthe and the other with the syrup. Refrigerate until required.

For The Iced Chocolate Parfait (Make The Day Before)

Place the sugar and water in a pan and boil to 118°C. Meanwhile, place the egg yolks in the bowl of a mixer and whisk until light and fluffy.

Slowly pour the boiling sugar onto the whisking egg yolks. Once all the sugar has been added, increase the speed and whisk until cool.

Thoroughly combine the egg mix into the melted chocolate. Finally, fold in the whipped cream. When all is mixed, pour gently into a container and place in the freezer overnight to set.

To Serve

Turn out the mosaic from the mould and slice. Garnish with the flavoured zest and a few pomegranate, passion fruit seeds and a little shredded mint. Scoop the parfait and arrange around the mosaic.

BBQ MACKEREL, ROASTED CUCUMBER, SOY & DILL DRESSING

SERVES 4

 Bordeaux Blanc
(France)

Ingredients

4 mackerel fillets (skin on, pin boned)
2 tbsp soy dressing
2 tbsp dill oil

Soy Dressing

2 cloves garlic
100ml rapeseed oil
30ml soy sauce
5ml nam pla fish sauce
100ml olive oil
20ml mirin

Dill Oil

100g fresh dill
200ml rapeseed oil

Tomatoes

8 baby heritage tomatoes
1-2 tbsp soy dressing

Cucumber

4 rectangular pieces of cucumber
8 ribbons of cucumber
salt
1-2 tbsp dill oil

Artichokes

4 baby globe artichokes (peeled)
1 tsp lemon juice

Garnish

salad leaves
olive oil caviar

barbecue and coals

Method

For The Soy Dressing (Make Ahead)

Mix the ingredients and gently warm the dressing to around 70°C for 3 hours and leave to infuse and cool.

For The Dill Oil (Make Ahead)

Blanch and refresh the dill then place into the oil and warm to around 70°C for 2 hours and leave to infuse.

To Prepare The Tomatoes

Blanch the tomatoes for 30 seconds in boiling water and refresh in cold water. Remove from the water and marinate in soy dressing for around 30 minutes.

For The Baby Artichokes

Cook the baby artichokes with the lemon juice in water for 12-15 minutes until soft. Cool in the liquid. When cool, halve and remove the choke from the centre. Place in with the tomatoes when ready to marinate.

For The Roast Cucumber

Cut the cucumber into four 10cm pieces and roast in a dry pan for 3 minutes to gain colour. Add some dill oil and cook for a further 3 minutes to soften. Do not overcook or they will become mushy.

To Make The Cucumber Ribbons

Peel the cucumber into ribbons with a peeler, salt for 2 minutes, pat dry and marinate in a little dill oil.

To Prepare The Mackerel

Marinate the mackerel in a mixture of dill oil and soy dressing before barbecuing. Cook over the coals for around 3-4 minutes making sure the fish does not overcook.

Chef's Tip

To get a really crispy skin on the mackerel without over cooking the fish, finish the skin with a blow torch. It also helps with the flavour.

To Finish

Place the mackerel on the plate and dress with the tomatoes and roasted cucumber. Roll the ribbons and finish the dish with the artichoke and a few leaves. Dress with both dill oil and soy dressing and some olive oil caviar.

ROAST WELSH BLACK BEEF RIBEYE, BRAISED OXTAIL, PEARL BARLEY, SAGE

SERVES 4

Cadillac Côtes de Bordeaux,
(France)

Ingredients

4 x 125g ribeye steaks (fat left on)

Braised Oxtail

½ oxtail
1 onion (chopped)
2 carrots (chopped)
1 stick celery (chopped)
250ml red wine
5g rosemary
5g thyme
water

Pearl Barley

100g pearl barley
50g shallot (finely chopped)
1 clove garlic (finely chopped)
10g mixed herbs (sage, rosemary, thyme)
50g butter
500ml water or good quality chicken stock
(to cover - top up as cooking - you may not
need all of it)

Sage Sauce

50g beef trimmings
2 shallots (finely chopped)
1 stick celery (chopped)
1 carrot (chopped)
10g sage
1 tbsp vegetable oil
100ml red wine
600ml veal or oxtail stock

To Serve

flour
4 banana shallots (pan roasted)
1 celeriac (cubed, pan roasted)
vegetables of your choice

500g terrine dish (lined with cling film)

Method

For The Braised Oxtail (Prepare The Day Before)

Brown the oxtail and the vegetables in a deep pan. *Deglaze* the
pan with the red wine and cover with water. Add the herbs and
simmer for 4 hours, topping up the water whilst cooking. When
cooked, remove from the pan and pick the meat from the bone.
Press into the terrine, leave to cool and set overnight in the fridge.

For The Pearl Barley

Melt the butter and sweat the shallot and garlic, add the herbs
and the barley, then cook for a further 2 minutes. Cover with the
chicken stock or water and simmer until cooked and soft,
roughly 20-30 minutes. When cooked, allow to cool in the liquid.

For The Sage Sauce

Brown the beef trimmings in a pan with a little oil, add the
vegetables and the sage. *Deglaze* with the red wine and reduce
slightly. Add the stock and reduce by half.

For The Beef

Oil and season the beef, pan fry in a dry hot pan for 3-4
minutes on each side. Allow to rest for 2 minutes, then cut
away fat before serving.

> **Chef's Tip**
>
> Pan fry the beef in a hot dry pan. Oil the meat not the pan
> to stop the beef from stewing and cook to no more than
> 57°C for a great steak. To help with the flavour, add a little
> butter when roasting.

To Serve

Warm the pearl barley with a little sage sauce and a touch of
butter. Cut the oxtail terrine into 3cm squares, flour lightly and
pan fry. Place the oxtail on the plate with the pearl barley, lay
the beef on top and finish with some shallots and celeriac or a
few vegetables of your choice. Lightly drizzle the sauce over and
around the beef.

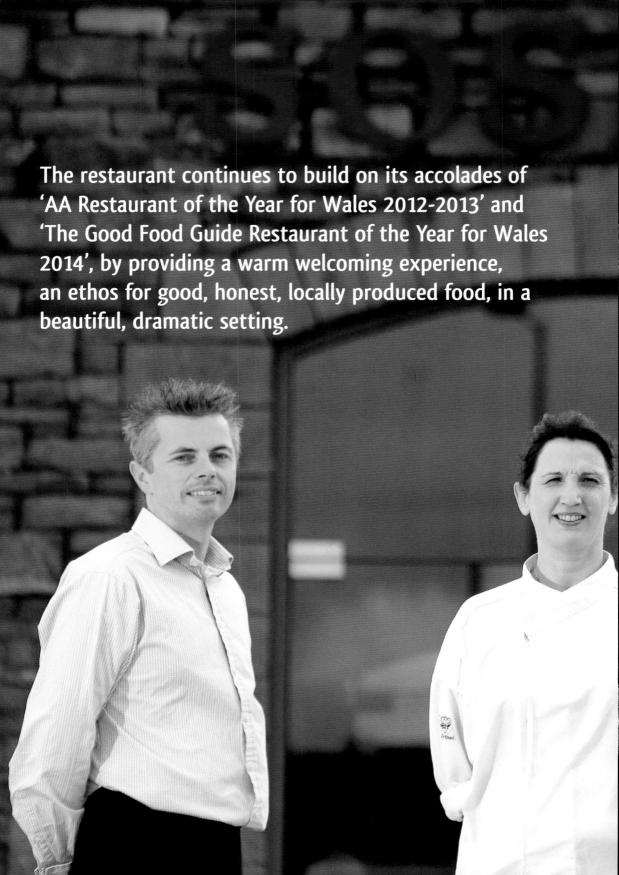

The restaurant continues to build on its accolades of 'AA Restaurant of the Year for Wales 2012-2013' and 'The Good Food Guide Restaurant of the Year for Wales 2014', by providing a warm welcoming experience, an ethos for good, honest, locally produced food, in a beautiful, dramatic setting.

LOBSTER CANNELLONI

SERVES 4

 Cool Coast Sauvignon Blanc, Casa Silva, Paredones Estate, 2010 (Chile)

Ingredients

The Pasta

250g '00' flour
3g salt
1 egg made up to 100ml with saffron stock
(saffron stock = 1½g saffron to 100ml of boiling water)

Shellfish Sauce

50g onions (chopped)
25g carrots (chopped)
25g leeks (sliced)
25g celery (sliced)
500g lobster and crab bones (roasted, crushed)
5g tomato purée
100ml brandy
250ml water
250ml cream
salt and pepper

The Mousse

100g salmon fillet
50g scallop white meat
1 egg white
200ml double cream
salt and pepper
1 x 400g lobster (cooked, meat picked and chopped)
parsley (chopped)

To Garnish

1 small bunch chervil (chopped)
1 small bunch chives (cut into batons)

Method

For The Pasta

Mix the flour and salt in a blender, then add the egg and saffron stock and blend until smooth. Rest the dough for at least 4 hours before using.

Roll the pasta on a pasta machine down to number 1. Roll twice on number 1 then cut into oblongs approximately 5cm by 12cm.

Blanch the pasta until just cooked in a pan of boiling salted water. Refresh in iced water.

Lay the cooked pasta onto an oiled tray, cover with cling film and keep refrigerated until you are ready to roll the cannelloni.

For The Shellfish Sauce

Sweat the onions, carrots, celery and leeks in a large pan without colouring, add the bones and brandy and flambé, then add the tomato purée and cook for 10 minutes. Cover with water and bring to the boil. Simmer for 20 minutes, pass through a sieve and return to the heat. Reduce by half, add the cream and reduce to required consistency. Season to taste.

> **Chef's Tip**
> You can make the pasta and sauce the day before to save you time.

For The Mousse

Purée the salmon and scallop meat in a blender until smooth, add the egg whites and season a little. Add the cream slowly then season to taste. Next add the chopped lobster meat and parsley. Place the mousse into a piping bag.

To Roll The Cannelloni

Place a sheet of cooked pasta onto a large sheet of cling film with a little olive oil, pipe one quarter of the mousse along the width, roll tightly and tie the cling film securely at both ends. Repeat 3 more times.

To Serve

Cook the cannelloni for 10 minutes in a pan of simmering water. Once cooked, remove from the cling film and serve with the warmed shellfish sauce. Garnish with a little chervil and chives.

PORK, PORK, PORK

SERVES 4

Los Gansos Pinot Noir 2012
(Chile)

Ingredients

Pork
300g pork belly
500g goose fat
300g pork fillet
100g pancetta (thinly sliced)
300g Trealy Farm black pudding (cut into 4
rectangular pieces)

Sauce
100g shallots (peeled, sliced)
100g carrots (peeled, chopped)
100ml brown chicken stock
100ml double cream
80g course grain mustard
20g tarragon (chopped)

Garnish
100g mashed potato
1 small Savoy cabbage (finely chopped, cooked)
200g baby spinach (washed, lightly *sautéed*)
1 Cox's Orange Pippin apple (quartered, peeled,
cored, caramelised in a knob of butter and a
sprinkling of sugar)

Method

To Cook The Pork Belly (Can Be Prepared The Day Before)

Preheat a fan oven to 100°C.

Place the belly in an ovenproof pan. Cover with goose fat, bring to the boil, then transfer into the oven for 3-4 hours or until the pork belly is cooked and tender. Allow to cool in the fat.

Once cool, remove the pork belly from the fat and cut into 4 even pieces. Reserve to one side.

> **Chef's Tip**
> Score the skin on the belly before cooking as this will help to give the skin a really good, crisp crackling.

To Prepare The Pork Fillet

Roll the pork fillet in the pancetta then set aside for serving.

To Make The Sauce

Sweat down the shallots and carrots in a pan until soft, add the stock and reduce to almost nothing. Add the cream and reduce a little. Finish by stirring through the grain mustard and tarragon. Season to taste.

When You Are Ready To Eat

Preheat a fan oven to 180°C.

Seal the pork fillet on all sides in a hot pan, then place in the oven for 8-10 minutes or until the fillet is cooked.

Seal the pork belly, skin side down, in a hot pan and cook in the oven for 8-10 minutes or until the belly is hot and the skin crispy.

Grill the black pudding until cooked.

To Serve

Place the mashed potato in the middle of the plate, place the cabbage to one side and the spinach on the other side.
Lay the black pudding on top of the potato along with the caramelised apple, place the pork belly on the cabbage and set the fillet on the spinach. Spoon the warmed sauce around and serve immediately.

MIXED BERRY CHEESECAKE

SERVES 4

Brown Brothers Late Harvest Muscat
(Australia)

Ingredients

Base

50g Hobnob biscuits
25g butter (melted)

Cheese Filling

200g cream cheese
100g icing sugar
1 vanilla pod (split in half, scrape out the seeds,
use the seeds only)
80ml double cream

Topping

100g macadamia nuts (roasted, chopped)

Sauce

100g caster sugar
100ml water
100g raspberries

To Finish

4 strawberries
8 raspberries
8 blueberries
8 blackberries

4 ring moulds 6cm wide by 5cm deep

Method

For The Base

Place the biscuits in a blender until a fine crumb. Add the butter until all incorporated. Put your moulds onto a tray lined with greaseproof paper. Evenly spread on the base of the 4 moulds.

For The Cheese Filling

Place the cream cheese, sugar and vanilla seeds into a mixer. Slowly add the cream until fully incorporated. Fill each of your moulds to the very top with the cheesecake mix, then smooth over the top with a palette knife. Allow to set in the fridge for at least 3 hours before using.

Chef's Tip

You can flavour the cheesecake with a fruit purée instead of vanilla.

To Make The Sauce

Place the sugar and water in a pan and bring to the boil. Reduce until you see small bubbles all over. Remove from the heat, add the raspberries, purée in a blender, pass through a sieve and allow to cool before serving.

To Finish

Take each cheesecake and cover the top with the macadamia nuts. De-mould onto one side of a round plate, arrange the fruit and sauce on the other side and serve.

230
TYDDYN LLAN

Llandrillo, Corwen, LL21 0ST

01490 440 264
www.tyddynllan.co.uk Twitter: @bryanwwebb

Susan and Bryan Webb have been at Tyddyn Llan, an elegant Georgian House on the edge of Snowdonia National Park, for 12 years. During this time they have built up a reputation for serving excellent food in elegant surroundings, which has gained them a Michelin star and constant high praise from the Good Food Guide. But if it's fancy food on a plate that you are looking for this is not the place, as Bryan cooks with sophisticated simplicity that embraces the best and most carefully sourced produce. The flavours are bold and to some, the portions are large, but remember we are in Wales. The kitchen at Tyddyn Llan follows Bryan's golden rules, buy the very best, following the seasons, cook them with love and care and keep it simple.

Bryan is a true Welshman born in Pontypool and brought up in the mining valleys while Susan, a Yorkshire lass, now feels more at home in Wales. Together they make the perfect husband and wife team. Susan's charm and ability ensures a smooth and professional service, creating a friendly and relaxing atmosphere while Bryan does what he does best - cooking in the kitchen.

Tyddyn Llan makes a perfect place for that special occasion with 12 luxury bedrooms and a ground floor Garden Suite for an overnight stay after indulging in its excellent wine list.

Relish Restaurant Rewards
See page 007 for details.

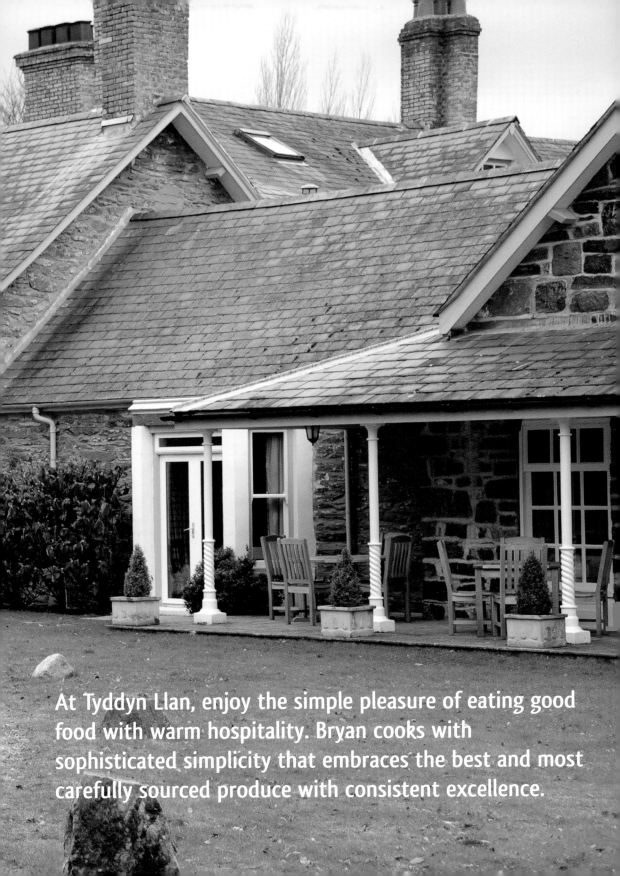

At Tyddyn Llan, enjoy the simple pleasure of eating good food with warm hospitality. Bryan cooks with sophisticated simplicity that embraces the best and most carefully sourced produce with consistent excellence.

SALAD OF PIG'S TROTTER WITH PICCALILLI

SERVES 4

 K-Naia 2012 Bodegas Naia, La Seca, Rueda (Spain)

Ingredients

2 pig's trotters (well cleaned, hairs removed)
1 ham hock
1 carrot (peeled, roughly chopped)
2 celery sticks (peeled, roughly chopped)
1 leek (peeled, roughly chopped)
1 onion (peeled, roughly chopped)
bouquet garni (thyme, parsley stalks, bay leaves
wrapped in a leek leaf and tied with string)
50g butter
1 small onion (finely chopped)
1 cup parsley (chopped)
100g fine white breadcrumbs
2 tbsp English mustard powder
2 eggs (beaten)
75g plain flour
salt and pepper

Vinaigrette (makes 750ml)

500ml olive oil
150ml walnut oil
100ml tarragon vinegar
½ tbsp mustard
10g salt
a few turns of black pepper

To Serve

apple purée
piccalilli
mixture of watercress, dandelion
and radicchio salads

Method

For The Pig's Trotters (Prepare The Day Before)

Place the trotters and ham hock in a large saucepan, cover with cold water and bring to the boil. Turn the heat down and skim all the scum that has come to the surface, continue to skim the surface for a further 10 minutes. Add the roughly chopped vegetables with the bouquet garni. Simmer for 3½ hours on a low heat.

Leave to cool in the pan. When cool enough to handle, remove from the liquid, shred the ham hock and place into a clean bowl, discarding the bones, gristle and the fat. Cut the trotters in half lengthways, remove the bones and mix the meat and fat with the ham hock.

Melt the butter in a small pan and cook the chopped onion until soft. Add to the ham mix with the chopped parsley.

Lay 2 large sheets of cling film on top of each other on a clean surface. Place the trotters' shins on the cling film opening them out and laying them flat and close to each other, lengthways.

Place the ham mixture onto the trotters to form a long sausage, then, using the cling film, roll as tight as possible. Twist the ends, tie with string and chill overnight.

The next day, mix the breadcrumbs and mustard powder together. Remove the cling film and cut 3 x 2cm discs. Cut each disc into quarters and coat in the flour, dip into the eggs and finally the breadcrumbs. There will some 'sausage' left over to use when serving.

> **Chef's Tip**
> Sometimes I cook the ham hock separately and use the stock with split yellow peas and diced root vegetables to make a real homely soup.

For The Vinaigrette

Place all the ingredients into a large bowl and mix well with a whisk, check the seasoning and keep in an airtight container.

I always keep some vinaigrette in a bottle with a lid on. Whenever I need some, I put my thumb on the neck and shake the bottle to control the flow onto the food.

To Serve

Heat a deep fat fryer to 180°C.

From the remaining 'sausage', thinly slice 12 slices of trotter and lay 3 slices on each plate. Add a teaspoon of apple purée on top of each slice and a teaspoon of piccalilli in between each slice.

Deep fry the coated trotter wedges until crisp and golden. Drain on kitchen paper, then place a piece on top of the apple purée. Dress the salad leaves with a little vinaigrette and arrange in the centre of the plate.

ROAST WILD BASS WITH LAVERBREAD BUTTER SAUCE

SERVES 4

 Saint-Veran 'Domaine des Deux Roches' 2012 (France)

Ingredients

Wild Bass

4 x 150g pieces wild bass
(skin on, pin bones removed)
1 tbsp olive oil
salt and pepper

Laverbread Butter Sauce

4 shallots (finely chopped)
1 tbsp white wine vinegar
175ml dry white wine (Muscadet if possible)
250g unsalted butter
salt and a pinch of cayenne pepper
½ lemon (juice of)
2 tbsp laverbread (type of seaweed - traditional
Welsh delicacy)
2 tbsp double cream

Spinach

300g raw picked spinach
50g butter

Method

For The Laverbread Butter Sauce

Start by making a *beurre blanc*. Put the white wine, vinegar and shallots into a saucepan and slowly reduce to a syrup.

On a low heat, slowly add the butter, stirring in a little at a time, until it forms a slightly thick sauce. Season with salt and cayenne pepper, add the lemon juice. Strain the sauce into a clean saucepan.

In a separate saucepan, add the laverbread with the cream, bring to the boil and add half the *beurre blanc*.

For The Sea Bass

Preheat the oven to 200°C (190°C fan).

Season the fish and coat lightly with olive oil. Gently put the bass onto a hot griddle pan, skin side down, until the skin is crisp. Place onto an oiled tray and bake in the oven for 5 minutes.

> **Chef's Tip**
> If you do not have a griddle pan, use a non-stick frying pan.

For The Spinach

While the fish is cooking, melt the butter in a large pan and cook the spinach until wilted.

To Serve

Serve the bass on a bed of spinach. Pour the laverbread sauce around one side and the remaining half of the *beurre blanc* around the other side.

PANNA COTTA

SERVES 6

🍷 *Mitchell Noble Semillon*
(Australia)

Method

For The Panna Cotta (Make The Day Before)

Put the cream, milk and vanilla pods into a large saucepan and slowly bring to the boil. Lower the heat and leave to simmer for 5 minutes.

Meanwhile, put the gelatine into cold water to soften, drain off the excess water.

Stir in the sugar and rum. Allow the sugar to dissolve. Remove from the heat and slip in the softened gelatine. Stir well and leave to cool.

Place 6 *dariole* moulds, small soup bowls or glass dishes, on a tray and pour the cold cream into the moulds.

Refrigerate overnight to set.

To Serve

Run a small knife around the moulds and place them in a bowl of boiling hot water for 10 seconds. Turn onto a cold plate and wait for it to go 'plop' out of the mould. It should be very delicate and wobbly.

Arrange the orange segments around each panna cotta and sprinkle the grappa over the top.

Ingredients

Panna Cotta

600ml double cream
150ml milk
2 vanilla pods (split in two lengthways)
150g caster sugar
2 tbsp rum (or Grappa)
3 leaves gelatine

To Serve

2 tbsp Grappa
6 blood oranges (cut into segments)

6 *dariole* moulds

240
THE WALNUT TREE

Llanddewi Skirrid, Abergavenny, Monmouthshire, NP7 8AW

01873 852 797
www.thewalnuttreeinn.com

The Walnut Tree stands on a B road, three miles outside Abergavenny. The look is that of a well-tended typical inn, however the reputation is of a world class restaurant. Integrity of ingredient and skill in the kitchen are the defining aspirations rather than the foams and squiggles of current food fashion. Everything served will be made on the premises, from bread and chocolates to black pudding and terrines.

Nothing in the restaurant world is free of course, except maybe the view. It is merely included, so the choices at any price point are a question of personal preference and value for money. The aims of the Walnut Tree will of course not appeal to everyone. Those wanting lots of napiery and chandeliers, needless bowing and scraping, will be disappointed for this is not where your money is spent. Those wanting excellence in cooking and an informal, but hopefully friendly and efficient, service will be considerably happier.

Most of the brigade of chefs have worked in the kitchen here under head chef Roger Brook since its takeover by Shaun Hill seven years ago.
The restaurant has won plenty of accolades, Michelin star, 3 AA Rosettes, and has been positively reviewed by every national newspaper. All this can be looked up online for a dispassionate opinion on what's on offer. The consensus so far though has been that it's worth a punt.

Relish Restaurant Rewards
See page 007 for details.

Hill has forged a unique style with a string of timeless dishes.

MONKFISH WITH GINGER, GARLIC & TOMATO

SERVES 4

 Gewürztraminer 2009 Kuehn
(France)

Ingredients

4 x 100g monkfish fillet
1 tbsp olive oil
butter (knob of)
seasoning (salt and pepper)
lemon juice (spritz of)

Salsa

1 tbsp vegetable oil
50g shallots (peeled, finely chopped)
50g fresh ginger (peeled, finely chopped)
4 cloves garlic (peeled, crushed)
1 small chilli (chopped)
1 tbsp tomato passata
2 tbsp white wine or stock (chicken or vegetable)
8 plum or beef tomatoes (skinned, deseeded,
cut into small dice)
50g unsalted butter
1 tbsp fresh coriander (chopped)
1 tbsp parsley (chopped)
½ lemon (juice of)

Method

For The Salsa

Warm the oil in a pan and gently cook the shallot, garlic, ginger and chilli so that they are cooked but not coloured.

Add a tablespoon of tomato passata (single strength tomato passata rather than the purée concentrate) and the stock or white wine.

Finally, add the fresh tomato, herbs and the butter. Stir until thickened then adjust the seasonings and spritz with lemon juice.

> **Chef's Tip**
> The sauce is a sort of warm salsa, fresh and lively to offset the pan fried fish, so don't cook it for too long. If you do, it will taste as good, but it will be more like a 'pizza topping'.

For The Fish

Heat the olive oil and butter in a large frying pan. When warm, fry the fish, season with salt, pepper and a spritz of lemon juice.

To Serve

Place a bed of warm sauce in the centre of your plate then carefully arrange the monkfish on top. Serve immediately.

SADDLE OF VENISON WITH FRESH GOAT'S CHEESE GNOCCHI

SERVES 4

 Givry 2011 Sarrazin
(France)

Method

To Make The Gnocchi

Preheat the oven to 180°C.

Heat the milk with some freshly grated nutmeg and seasoning, then stir in the semolina. Bring to the boil stirring continuously. Still stirring, add the egg followed by the Parmesan.

Pour half the mixture into the ovenproof dish. Add a layer of the sliced goat's cheese, then cover the cheese with the remaining gnocchi mixture. Bake until firm, but still with a little give, for about 20 minutes.

For The Venison

Brush the boned venison with olive oil. Sear in a hot pan and roast until pink for about 15 minutes at 180°C. Remove from the oven, keep warm and allow the venison to relax.

To Serve

With the oven still at 180°C, cut the gnocchi into bite sized squares. Heat a little oil in an ovenproof pan and when hot, add the gnocchi. Transfer the pan containing the gnocchi to the oven and bake for 15 minutes.

Slice and plate the venison. Turn the gnocchi over so that the crisp side is uppermost and drizzle round with the pan juices.

Chef's Tip
Allow about 175g filleted weight of venison per person.

Ingredients

700g saddle of venison (boned)
oil for greasing

Gnocchi

500ml milk
nutmeg (freshly grated)
salt and pepper
150g semolina
25g Parmesan cheese (grated)
1 egg (beaten)
100g fresh goat's cheese (sliced)
oil for greasing

20cm square ovenproof dish (greased)

BUTTERMILK PUDDING WITH BAKED CARDAMOM FIGS

SERVES 6

 Beerenauslese 2008 Willi Opitz
(Austria)

Ingredients

Buttermilk Pudding

200ml double cream
250g caster sugar
1 vanilla pod (split)
4 strips orange peel
½ lemon (juice of)
3 leaves gelatine (soaked in cold water)
600ml buttermilk
200ml whipped cream

Figs

9 figs (halved)
1 tbsp caster sugar
1 tsp cardamom seeds (crushed)
1 orange (juice of)
1 tbsp clear honey

Garnish

shortbread or any crisp biscuit

6 *dariole* moulds or ramekins

Method

For The Buttermilk Pudding (Make The Day Before)

Bring the double cream, sugar, vanilla and orange peel to the boil. Remove from the heat then add lemon juice and softened gelatine. Strain into a clean jug. Pour the buttermilk into a large bowl then gradually whisk in the hot cream. Cool the mixture and when cold, fold in the whipped cream. Spoon the mix into *dariole* moulds or ramekins and refrigerate overnight.

To Bake The Cardamom Figs

Preheat the oven to 180°C.

Arrange the figs in a single layer in a baking dish and sprinkle over the cardamom, sugar, orange juice and honey. Bake until hot, approximately 8-10 minutes, then remove from the oven.

To Serve

Place 3 fig halves to the side of each buttermilk pudding then finish with a little cooking liquor. Serve with shortbread or any crisp biscuit.

250 WOLFSCASTLE COUNTRY HOTEL

Haverfordwest, Pembrokeshire, SA62 5LZ

01437 741 225
www.wolfscastle.com Twitter: @staywolfscastle

Wolfscastle Country Hotel is situated in the village of Wolfscastle, only 10 minutes from the beautiful Pembrokeshire coastline, and has been synonymous with good food for 36 years.

'I bought the property in 1976 - an old vicarage and developed my two passions, food and the game of squash.

Good food was something I grew up with, my parents owning the Hat and Feather in Knutsford which in 1966, was voted by the Good Food Guide one of the best 20 restaurants in Britain. With squash, I had been lucky enough to go to a school which had squash courts and developed a passion for the game, building two courts onto the side of the hotel - now converted to bedrooms. Last year we built a contemporary brasserie at the front of the hotel, designed by my wife Mandy aided by an interior designer. We named it the 'Allt-yr-Afon' Brasserie - the original name of the house.

The restaurant, along with the brasserie, gives Tom Simmons, our exciting head chef and his brigade of six, plenty of scope to develop traditional as well as fine dining dishes. As a recent visitor on Trip Advisor said "We have been visiting this hotel for food and the occasional overnight stay for over 10 years now. It is the best dining experience for miles - delicious meals, great care and attention given by the management and the friendly staff to every detail, and great ambience. Recent extensions have enlarged the hotel and bar by clever use of space, and to the customary high standards. A delight to visit!!"

Tom, who came to us via Claridges, Le Gallois and cooking in France, reached the quarter finals of MasterChef: The Professionals in 2011. He is an inspiration to us, bringing his enthusiasm and love of cooking to the hotel, creating traditional as well as classic dishes.'

Andrew Stirling, Proprietor

Relish Restaurant Rewards
See page 007 for details.

Winners of The AA Restaurant of the Year and The Good Food Guide Readers Recommended Restaurant for Wales. Of course the awards are nice but Mark and Sue are more proud that they continue to satisfy the appetites of their loyal regular guests and the new friends discovering Y Polyn for the first time.

HARE TORTELLINI, ONION SOUBISE, DEEP FRIED SAGE

SERVES 4

🍷 *Château Haut Peyrous 2010, Blanc, Marc Darroze, Graves (France)*

Ingredients

Pasta

550g '00' flour
3 whole eggs
8 egg yolks
1 egg (beaten for egg wash)

Onion *Soubise*

2 large onions (finely sliced)
125g butter
2 bay leaves
1 small bunch sage (reserve 16 nice leaves,
for the deep fried garnish)
salt and pepper

Hare Ragû

1 wild hare (jointed, seasoned)
2 tbsp oil (to brown the hare)
200g smoked pancetta (skin removed, finely diced)
4 carrots (peeled, 2 roughly chopped,
2 finely chopped)
4 stalks celery (2 roughly chopped,
2 finely chopped)
2 large onions (1 roughly chopped,
1 finely chopped)
4 bay leaves
small bunch thyme
1 star anise
2 heaped tbsp tomato purée
1 bottle red wine
1 litre veal or chicken stock
150ml ruby port
1 bulb garlic (finely chopped)

Garnish

Parmesan shavings

large cake cutter to shape the pasta

Method

To Make The Hare Ragû And Sauce (Prepare The Day Before)

Preheat the oven to 160°C.

Seal the hare in a heavy based casserole pan, remove then add the roughly chopped vegetables. Cook until golden, add bay leaves, thyme, star anise and half the tomato purée. Add half the red wine and reduce by half. Return the hare to the casserole and cover with stock. Bring to the boil then transfer to the oven for about 2 hours until the meat is falling from the bones. Strain off the juices, carefully pick the meat from the bones and set aside. Discard the bones.

Cook the pancetta in a heavy bottomed pan until golden. Strain off the excess fat. Add the garlic and remaining vegetables and cook gently until soft. Add the remaining half of the tomato purée, stir well, then add the port and remaining wine. Reduce by half. Add half the strained cooking juices and simmer. Reduce the remaining cooking liquor to a coating consistency for saucing the plates.

Combine the meat with the vegetable and sauce mixture. Cook until it is fairly dry to make your pasta stuffing. Check for seasoning and allow the mix to get cold in the fridge.

For The Pasta

Sieve the flour onto a clean work surface. Make a well in the centre and add the eggs. Bring the mixture together to create a smooth dough and knead for 10 minutes. Wrap in cling film and rest for an hour in the fridge. Cut the dough into 4 pieces and feed through a pasta machine on the thinnest setting. Using a large round cake cutter, cut circles from the pasta leaves, egg washing the edges and fill with around 25g of hare mix. Seal the half moons of pasta carefully being sure to exclude all air. Dexterously whirl them around your little finger to make tortellini shapes (easier said than done!) Reserve 12, freeze the rest.

> **Chef's Tip**
> Don't stuff the pasta until the filling mix is cold.

For The *Soubise*

Cook the onions slowly in a heavy bottomed pan with the bay leaves, butter and 6 large sage leaves. Cover with a greaseproof paper disc and stir occasionally until the onions are very soft and translucent but have not coloured. Season to taste, remove the herbs.

To Serve

Warm the onion mix, cook the pasta in a large pot of boiling salted water for 2 minutes. Drop the tortellini into the onion mix and coat with the sauce. Plate 3 tortellini per person, drizzle on the hare sauce, garnish with deep fried sage leaves and Parmesan shavings.

ROAST WOOD PIGEON BREAST, CHESTNUTS, SQUASH & CAVOLO NERO

SERVES 4

 Chateauneuf du Pape 'Les Cailloux' 2010 Lucien and André Brunel (France)

Ingredients

4 wood pigeons (breasts removed and bones reserved)
250g wild mushrooms (dried)
250ml red wine
250ml ruby port
1 tbsp tomato purée

The Sauce

2 onions (chopped)
2 carrots (chopped)
2 sticks celery (chopped)
2 bulbs garlic (chopped)
2 leeks (chopped)
4 sprigs thyme
2 stalks rosemary
2 bay leaves
50g butter (cold, diced, to finish)

Squash

2 butternut squash (peeled, diced)
250g butter
200ml milk
200ml double cream

Garnish

250g cavolo nero
1 large red chilli (finely chopped)
3 cloves garlic (chopped)
250g chestnut mushrooms (quartered, *sautéed* in 50g butter)
250g cooked chestnuts (lightly toasted under a hot grill)

Method

For The Pigeon And The Sauce

Roast the pigeon bones until golden. Sweat off the vegetables and herbs for the sauce until softened and golden. Add the bones and dried mushroom mix, add the wine and port then reduce by half. Add tomato purée, cover with water and bring to the boil. Turn the mixture down to a low simmer and cook for about 2 hours. Strain the mixture and reduce by three quarters until you have a glossy sauce. Reserve until you assemble the dish.

For The Squash Purée

Preheat the oven to 180°C.

Bake the squash until tender, approximately 20 minutes. Heat the butter, milk and cream in a pan, add the squash. Reduce the mixture until the squash is soft and half the volume of liquid remains. Liquidise the mixture in a blender and season to taste. Reserve.

To Assemble The Dish

Preheat the oven to 180°C.

Season the pigeon breasts with salt and pepper and cook in a hot pan, skin side down for about 30 seconds. Turn the breasts over and remove the hot pan from the heat. The residual heat will cook the breasts. You want them rare or medium rare, no further or they will dry out. Rest the cooked breasts.

Trim the cavolo nero, *blanch* in boiling, salted water then refresh in iced water. Sweat off the chilli and garlic until soft, then add the cavolo nero to reheat.

Heat up the squash purée in a pan, and the chestnuts and mushrooms in the oven. Slowly add the butter to the sauce as you warm it in a pan, whisking well and check for seasoning. Assemble the dish as per the photograph.

> **Chef's Tip**
> Rest the breasts well after cooking, they'll be much juicier.

RHUBARB & CUSTARD

SERVES 4

 *Michele Chiarlo Nivole, Moscato d'Asti 2012
(Italy)*

Ingredients

Rhubarb Jelly

600g rhubarb (washed, trimmed, finely sliced)
200g caster sugar
1 tbsp grenadine
4 leaves gold gelatine

Panna Cotta

4 leaves gold gelatine
2 vanilla pods (split, seeds scraped out)
150g caster sugar
150ml milk
600ml double cream

Poached Rhubarb And Syrup

200g caster sugar
1 litre water
2 tbsp grenadine
3 sticks rhubarb (washed, trimmed, cut into
5cm lengths)

moulds for setting (see method for options)

Method

For The Rhubarb Jelly

Place the rhubarb, sugar and grenadine in a heat proof bowl and cover with cling film. Sit over a pan of gently simmering water for about 2 hours until lots of juice has been released. Strain the liquid through muslin into a measuring jug. Soak the gelatine in cold water until it is soft and pliable and whisk into the warm rhubarb liquid. Pour into moulds and chill until set. You can set the jelly in individual moulds or in a deep tray lined with cling film. Fill your moulds no more than about one third.

For The Panna Cotta

Soak the gelatine in cold water until soft and pliable. Place the vanilla pods and seeds, sugar, milk and cream into a saucepan and heat gently until the sugar has dissolved. Bring to the boil and take off the heat. Squeeze the gelatine leaves to remove excess water and whisk into the milk mixture. Strain through a sieve into a bowl set over iced water and whisk until cold but not yet set. Pour the cold mixture over the set jelly in your moulds and leave to set in the fridge.

For The Poached Rhubarb And Syrup

Poach the rhubarb gently in a stock made from the water, sugar and grenadine, taking care not to overcook. Remove from the liquid and reserve. Reduce the liquid to a light syrup for the sauce and leave both to cool. Assemble your dish as pictured.

> **Chef's Tip**
> Make sure the panna cotta and jelly are both cold before combining them. You can make all elements of this dish the day before.

WALES SECOND HELPING LARDER

FISH

SWANSEA FISH LTD

Unit 5, Fisherman's Quay, Trawler Road, The Marina, Swansea, SA1 1UN
T: 01792 480 800
www.swanseafish.net

Freshly caught fish direct to your dish. Supplied as fresh or frozen.

WELSH SEAFOOD

The Docks, Milford Haven, Pembrokeshire, SA73 3AE
T: 01646 692 331
www.welshseafoods.co.uk

Suppliers of Welsh fish to local restaurants, building a recognisable brand for fish caught in Welsh waters and landed on Welsh shores.

FINE FOOD & VEGETABLES

A DAVID & CO LTD

Hillside Farm, Sutton Wick, Bishop Sutton, Bristol, BS39 5XR
T: 0844 120 555
www.adavid.co.uk

A food service distribution company supplying the catering industry for over 50 years.

CASTELL HOWELL FOODS LTD

Cross Hands Food Park, Cross Hands, Llanelli, Carmarthenshire, SA14 6SX
T: 01269 846 060
www.chfoods.co.uk

Distributors of fine foods and local produce, working with the best producers in Wales.

WILD FOODS 365

T: 07717 780 411
www.wildfood365.co.uk

Henry Ashby has been foraging for over 50 years for the likes of James Sommerin and many others.

Angela Gray's

Cookery School

at Llanerch Vineyard

Angela Gray's Cookery School is situated in the wonderful surroundings of Llanerch Vineyard in the beautiful Vale of Glamorgan.

Offering a range of courses and events including full one day courses, skill builder courses, master classes, 'Cookstart' courses for young foodies and bespoke events for friends, hens and corporate team building days. The school runs a monthly lunch club, an evening chef's table and many bespoke cookery days. The monthly Saturday Morning Kitchen demonstration event is an opportunity to view the school and the rest of Llanerch whilst watching Angela cook some fabulously simple but impressive and flavoursome dishes.

Llanerch Vineyard, Hensol, Vale of Glamorgan, CF72 8GG
Telephone 01443 222 716
www.llanerch-vineyard.co.uk www.angelagray.co.uk
Twitter: @AGrayCookery facebook.com/angelagraycookery

MEAT

EYNON'S OF ST CLEARS LTD

Deganwy, Pentre Road, St Clears, Carmarthen, SA33 4LR
T: 01994 230 226
www.eynons.co.uk

Huw Eynon is one of the most skilful butchers in Wales and his excellent shop and food hall should be a stop on every foodie's itinerary on a visit to Carmarthenshire.

HUNTSHAM COURT FARM

Huntsham Court, Ross-on-Wye, Herefordshire, HR9 6JN
T: 01600 890 296
www.huntsham.com
E: Richard@huntsham.com

Richard Vaughan's farm produces some of the finest rare breed meats including pork, beef and lamb.

T J ROBERTS & SON

Tryweryn House, 8 Station Road, Bala, Gwynedd, LL23 7NG
T: 01678 520 471
www.welshqualitymeat.co.uk

Excellent award-winning family butcher supplying local Welsh black beef, pork and lamb.

THE WELSH VENISON CENTRE

Bwlch, Brecon, Powys, LD3 7SZ
T: 01874 730 929
www.beaconsfarmshop.co.uk

Excellent free range venison and lamb situated in the heart of the Brecon Beacons National Park. Family run farm shop since 1985.

DAIRY

BIRCHGROVE EGGS

Trawscoed, Aberystwyth, Ceredigion, SY23 4AT
T: 01974 261 286
www.birchgrove-eggs.co.uk

At Birchgrove they only have healthy and happy hens, with acres of land for them to roam and explore. They produce truly eggsellent eggs so everyone's a winner! A family run business supplying quality assured, Welsh free range eggs to a wide range of customers in Wales.

CALON WEN

Unit 8 West Wales Business Park, Redstone Road,
Narberth, Pembrokeshire, SA67 7ES
T: 01834 862 873
www.calonwen-cymru.com

The Welsh Organic Milk Co-Op. An organic dairy co-operative of organic family farms, located all over Wales.

PERL LAS BLUE CHEESE

Caws Cenarth, Fferm Glyneithinog, Pontseli, Lancych,
Carmarthenshire, SA37 0LH
T: 01239 710 432
www.cawscenarth.co.uk

Award-winning family run business with a six generation tradition of cheese making.

GLOSSARY

AL DENTE
Al dente describes vegetables that are cooked to the 'tender crisp' phase - still offering resistance to the bite, but cooked through. Al dente can also describe cooked pasta which is firm but not hard.

BAIN-MARIE
A pan or other container of hot water with a bowl placed on top of it. This allows the steam from the water to heat the bowl so ingredients can be gently heated or melted.

BEURRE BLANC
French translates as 'white butter'. A hot emulsified butter sauce made with a reduction of vinegar and/or white wine (normally Muscadet) and grey shallots. Cold, whole butter is blended off the heat to prevent separation.

BEURRE NOISETTE
Literally translates as hazelnut butter, but loosely as brown butter. It is frequently used in French pastry production. It can also be used as a warm sauce to accompany many foods, such as winter vegetables, pasta, fish, omelettes and chicken.

BLANCH
Boiling an ingredient before removing it and plunging it in ice cold water in order to stop the cooking process.

CHINOIS
A conical sieve with an extremely fine mesh. It is used to strain custards, purées, soups and sauces, producing a very smooth texture.

CLARIFIED BUTTER
Milk fat rendered from butter to separate the milk solids and water from the butter fat.

CONCASSE
To rough chop any ingredient, usually vegetables, most specifically applied to tomatoes, with tomato concasse being a tomato that has been peeled and seeded (seeds and skins removed).

CONFIT
A method of cooking where the meat is cooked and submerged in a liquid to add flavour. Often this liquid is rendered fat. Confit can also apply to fruits - fruit confits are cooked and preserved in sugar, the result is like candied fruits.

DARIOLE
A French term that refers to small, cylinder shaped moulds.

DEGLAZE
A fancy term for using the flavour-packed brown bits stuck to the bottom of a pan to make a sauce or gravy.

ECRASEE
French for crushed.

EMULSION/EMULSIFY
In the culinary arts, an emulsion is a mixture of two liquids that would ordinarily not mix together, like oil and vinegar.

JULIENNE
A culinary knife cut in which the vegetable is cut into long thin strips, similar to matchsticks.

JUS
The natural juices given off by the food.

PANE
To coat with flour, beaten egg and breadcrumbs for deep frying.

QUENELLE (OR ROCHER)
A finely minced fish or meat mixture formed into small portions, poached in stock and served in a sauce, or as a garnish to other dishes. The term is also used to describe their characteristic shape - a neat, three-sided oval (resembling a mini rugby ball) that is formed by gently smoothing the mixture between two dessert spoons. A quenelle shape can also be formed from other foods such as chocolate mousse.

SAUTE
To fry in a small amount of fat.

SOUBISE
A purée of onions mixed into a thick white sauce.

VELOUTE
A rich white sauce or soup made from stock, egg yolks and cream.

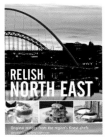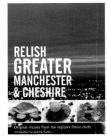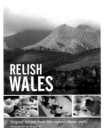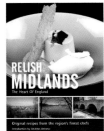

  Download your FREE sample pages now from the App Store/Relish Cookbook.

Apple, the Apple logo and iPhone are trademarks of Apple Inc, registered in the US and other countries, App Store is a service mark of Apple Inc.

BEST OF BRITISH

Relish Publications is an independent publishing house offering an exclusive insight into Britain's finest restaurants and chefs through their series of award-winning recipe books.

Each book contains signature recipes from your favourite chefs, recommended wines, stunning food photography and an impressive guide to each participating restaurant, plus a larder featuring the region's best produce suppliers. These ingredients make the Relish series an ultimate 'foodies' guide for individuals wishing to dine in great restaurants or create outstanding recipes at home.

The series of beautiful hard back recipe books is available to buy in the featured restaurants, all good bookshops and online at the Relish bookshop or on Amazon.

For more information please visit **www.relishpublications.co.uk**

Relish PUBLICATIONS

Duncan and Teresa Peters founded Relish Publications in 2009, through a passion for good food, a love of publishing and after recognising the need to promote the fantastic chefs and restaurants each region in the UK has to offer.
Relish Publications also specialise in bespoke cookbooks for individual chefs.

Since launching, their goal was simple. Create beautiful books with high quality contributors (each edition features a selection of the region's top chefs) to build a unique and invaluable recipe book.

As recipe book specialists, their team works with hundreds of chefs personally to ensure each edition exceeds the readers' expectations.

Thank you for Relishing with us!

HERE'S WHAT SOME OF BRITAIN'S BEST CHEFS HAVE SAID ABOUT WORKING WITH RELISH

"The Relish team has truly been amazing to work with. To have produced my book within two months from start to finish, only shows how professional a team of people can be."
Jean-Christophe Novelli

"The Relish cookbook offers the home cook some great inspiration to make the most of these wonderful ingredients in season." *Tom Kitchin, The Kitchin, Edinburgh*

"With mouth-watering, easy to follow recipes and beautiful photography, this book is a must have for any foodie, from professional chef to the inspired home cook"
Michael Caines MBE

"Relish brings together some of the most talented chefs from the regions. It shines the spotlight on the exceptional ways in which fresh, seasonal, local ingredients are put to good use." *Gary Jones, Executive Head Chef, Le Manoir aux Quat'Saisons*

CONVERSION CHART

COOKING TEMPERATURES

Degrees Celsius	Fahrenheit	Gas Mark
140	275	1
150	300	2
160–170	325	3
180	350	4
190	375	5
200–210	400	6
220	425	7
230	450	8
240	475	9

*Temperatures for fan-assisted ovens are, as a general rule, normally about 20°C lower than regular oven temperature. In this book, all temperatures stated are for conventional (non-fan) ovens, unless otherwise specified.

WEIGHT MEASUREMENT CONVERSIONS

1 teaspoon (5ml/5g)	$^1/_4$ oz
1 tablespoon (15ml/15g)	$^3/_4$ oz
10g	$^1/_2$ oz
25g	1oz
50g	2oz
75g	3oz
150g	5oz
200g	7oz
250g	9oz
350g	12oz
450g	1lb
1kg	2.2lb

VOLUME MEASUREMENT CONVERSIONS

55ml	2 fl oz
150ml	$^1/_4$ pt
275ml	$^1/_2$ pint
570ml	1 pt
1 litre	$1^3/_4$ pt